Dealing with Terrorism – Stick or Carrot?

Dealing with Terrorism – Stick or Carrot?

Bruno S. Frey

Professor of Economics, University of Zurich, Switzerland

Edward Elgar

Cheltenham, UK • Northampton, MA, USA

Published by
Edward Elgar Publishing Limited
Glensanda House
Montpellier Parade
Cheltenham
Glos GL50 1UA
UK

Edward Elgar Publishing, Inc.
136 West Street
Suite 202
Northampton
Massachusetts 01060
USA

A catalogue record for this book
is available from the British Library

Library of Congress Cataloguing in Publication Data
Frey, Bruno S.
    Dealing with terrorism : stick or carrot? / by Bruno S. Frey.
        p. cm.
    Includes bibliographical references.
        1. Terrorism – Prevention. 2. Terrorism – Economic aspects.
    3. Terrorism – Social aspects.
    I. Title

HV6431.F724 2004
363.32–dc22   2004046961

ISBN 1 84376 828 3 (cased)

Printed and bound in Great Britain by MPG Books Ltd, Bodmin, Cornwall

Contents

Contents

Introduction: The Failure of Deterrence and the Prospects of Positive Anti-terrorist Policies

This book provides a critique of deterrence policy; that is, the use of the stick, to fight terrorism. Coercion or negative sanctions are found to have little effect and, in important instances, are even counterproductive. The same holds, on the whole, for economic sanctions imposed on countries supporting terrorists. Using coercion is useful only under very specific conditions. This conclusion stands in stark contrast to the anti-terrorist policy undertaken all over the world.

It is therefore important to seriously consider alternative anti-terrorist policies going beyond coercion. Such an alternative view is presented here. Most importantly, the book demonstrates that there are viable and effective policies using a positive approach, that is, using carrots, to fight terrorism. Three specific anti-terrorist policies are proposed.

POLYCENTRICITY OR DECENTRALISATION REDUCES VULNERABILITY TO TERRORIST ATTACKS

A system with many different centres is more stable due to its diversity, enabling one part to substitute for another. When one part of the system is negatively affected, one or several other parts may take over. Polycentricity is effective in reducing risk and uncertainty. This basic insight also applies to terrorism. A target's vulnerability is lower in a polycentric society than in a centralised society. The more centres of power there are in a country, the less terrorists are able to harm it. In a decentralised system, terrorists do not know where to attack because they are aware that one part can substitute for another so that the attack will not achieve as much.

In contrast, in a centralised system, most decision-making power with respect to the economy, polity and society is to be found in one location. This power centre makes an ideal target for terrorists and therefore is in great danger of being attacked. This creates huge costs. If the centre is targeted and hit, the whole decision-making structure collapses, promoting chaos.

A prospective target of terrorist attacks can reduce its vulnerability by implementing various forms of decentralisation:

- *The economy*, by relying on the market as the major form of decentralised resource allocation. It refers to both decision-making as well as space;
- *The polity*, by resorting to the classical division of power between government, parliament and courts. Decentralisation of space is achieved by a federalistic structure, with decision-making power delegated to lower levels of the polity (states, provinces, regions and communes);
- *The society*, by allowing for many different actors, such as churches, non-governmental organisations, clubs and other units.

POSITIVE INCENTIVES CAN BE OFFERED TO ACTUAL AND PROSPECTIVE TERRORISTS NOT TO ENGAGE IN VIOLENT ACTS

Positive sanctions consist in providing people with previously non-existing or unattainable opportunities, thereby increasing their utility. The *opportunity costs* of being a terrorist are raised because other valued possibilities are now available. Various approaches are possible:

- *Reintegrating terrorists.* One of the most fundamental human motivations is the need to belong. This also applies to terrorists. The isolation from other social entities gives strength to the terrorist group because it has become the only place where the sense of belonging is nurtured. An effective way of dealing with terrorism is to break up this isolation. The (potential) terrorists need to experience that there are other social bodies able to provide them with a sense of belonging. Interaction between groups tends to reduce extremist views. Extremist views are more likely to flourish in isolated groups of like-minded people. Segregation reinforces extremism and vice versa. Breaking up this vicious circle of segregation and extremism can therefore be expected to lower the propensity of terrorists to participate in violent activities.

There are various ways of motivating terrorists to interact more closely with other members of society and thereby to overcome their isolation. The terrorists can be involved in a *discussion process*, which takes their goals and grievances seriously and tries to see whether compromises are feasible. Moreover, terrorists can be granted access to the normal *political process*. This lowers the costs of pursuing the political goal by legal means and hence raises the opportunity costs of terrorism.

The same principle of anti-terrorist policy can be applied to nations supporting or harbouring terrorists. If such countries are internationally isolated and identified as 'rogue states', large sections of the population tend to become radicalised. A more fruitful strategy is to help them re-enter the international community and adopt its rules.

- *Welcoming repentents.* Persons engaged in terrorist movements can be offered various incentives, such as reduced punishment and a secure future life if they are ready to leave the organisation they are involved with and are prepared to talk about it and its projects. Terrorists who genuinely show that they wish to renounce terrorist activities should be supported and not penalised. The opportunity costs of remaining a terrorist are thereby increased.
- *Offering valued opportunities.* Persons inclined to follow terrorist ideas and undertake terrorist actions can be invited to visit foreign countries. Universities and research institutes, for example, can offer such persons the opportunity of discussing their ideology with intellectuals. It is to be expected that being faced with the liberal ideas existing in such places of learning will mellow their terrorist inclinations. At the very least, the (potential) terrorists have access to new and radically different ideas, compared with the situation in which they live within a closed circle of other terrorists.

Precisely this point constitutes an argument in favour of open markets and against economic sanctions that restrict the opportunities available for individuals in target countries.

DIVERT ATTENTION FROM THE TERRORIST GROUPS

The relationship between terrorists and the media has been described as 'symbiotic', which means that it is mutually advantageous. The interests of the terrorists are similar, or even identical, to those of the media. Both want to make news, and both want to keep the incident in the headlines for as long as possible.

Terrorists have become very skilled in using the media to achieve maximum effect. They have learned what the media need to propagate their political demands to millions and even billions of people. Terrorists have started to change their tactics in order to accommodate media needs.

Terrorists can be prevented from committing violent acts by reducing the amount of utility they gain from such behaviour. A specific way for terrorists to derive lower benefits from terrorism would be for the government to ascertain that a particular terrorist act is *not attributed to a particular terrorist group*. This prevents terrorists from receiving credit for the act and thereby gaining the full publicity for having committed it. The government must see to it that the terrorist act and the corresponding media attention are not monopolised by a particular terrorist group.

Diffusing media attention can be achieved by the government supplying *more* information to the public than the terrorist group responsible for a particular violent act would wish. It must be made known that one of several terrorist groups *could* be responsible for a particular terrorist act. The authorities have to reveal that they never know with absolute certainty which terrorist group may have committed a violent act. Even when it seems glaringly obvious which terrorist group is involved, the police can never be sure. The government should openly discuss various reasonable hypotheses.

The information strategy of refusing to attribute a terrorist attack to one particular group systematically affects the behaviour of terrorists. The benefits derived from having committed a terrorist act decrease for the group that has undertaken it because it does not reap the much hoped for public attention. The political goals the group wants to publicise are not propagated as much as they would have liked. This reduction in publicity makes the terrorist act (to a certain extent) pointless, as modern terrorism essentially depends on publicity. Terrorists who are ready to risk their lives in order to broadcast their political beliefs feel deeply dissatisfied. The frustration is intensified by the feeling that other political groups not 'courageous' enough to run the risk of undertaking terrorist acts profit from free riding. This frustration can be intense because terrorist groups tend to be in a state of strong competition with one another, even when they have similar political beliefs.

Providing terrorists with positive incentives or 'carrots' to no longer engage in violent actions represents a completely different approach from the conventional anti-terrorist policy of deterrence based on coercion, or 'the stick'. My proposals seek to break the organisational and mental dependence of persons on the terrorist organisations by offering them more favourable alternatives. They are given an incentive for relinquishing terrorism. Deterrence policy does exactly the opposite: terrorists are locked into their organisation even more and see no alternatives but to stay on.

The proposed anti-terrorist policy based on a *positive approach* has two important advantages over a coercive policy. First, and most importantly, the whole interaction between terrorists and the government transforms into a *positive sum game*: both sides benefit. The government's effort is no longer directed towards destruction. Rather, the government makes an effort to raise the utility of those terrorists who choose to enter the programmes on offer. It provides alternatives to persons considering engaging in terrorism. In contrast, deterrence policy of necessity produces a situation where both sides stand to lose. The terrorists are punished (incarcerated, killed, etc.), while the government often has to raise large sums of money to fund their deterrence strategy.

Secondly, the strategy undermines the cohesiveness of the terrorist organisation. The incentive to leave is an ever present threat to the organisation. The terrorist leaders no longer know whom to trust because, after all, most persons can succumb to temptation. An effort to counteract these temptations by prohibiting members from taking up the attractive offers leads to conflicts between leaders and rank-and-file members. With good outside offers available to the members of a terrorist group, its leaders tend to lose control. The terrorist organisation's effectiveness is thereby reduced.

This book intends to show the advantages of using an *economic approach* when analysing terrorism. This point of view differs markedly from the stance taken in political science, sociology or psychology. These latter approaches tend to dominate the field, while the economic view tends to be neglected. According to the economic approach, people act in a rational way. This also applies to potential and actual terrorists. They compare the benefits and costs of alternative actions. When the benefits of their undertaking a terrorist act increase, they engage more fully or more often. When the costs of their undertaking a terrorist act rise, they decide to undertake such terrorist acts less and look for alternative measures to make their political discontent known.

The economic approach to terrorism might be used to argue that only the threat of punishment and death induces terrorists to refrain from their activities. As will be shown, however, such reasoning is superficial and misleading. In particular, it reflects the fact that a deterrence policy creates substantial additional economic and political costs, increases vulnerability to terrorist acts, and strengthens terrorists' cohesiveness and influence. Fighting terrorism by governmental counter-terror thus involves heavy costs, going far beyond the clearly visible budgetary outlays. Deterrence moreover induces terrorists to switch their activities to other areas and other kinds of terrorism that are more difficult to control.

The application of the economic approach to terrorism offers a wide range of anti-terrorism policies which are superior to deterrence. They are effective in dissuading potential terrorists from attacking. The positive approach championed here is not the only strategy and it does not work in every case. But, compared with the currently predominant deterrence policy, the favourable features by far prevail. There is no need to restrict deterrence policies; the positive approaches presented are in many respects better alternatives.

A crucial question is why deterrence policy is so often undertaken, although it is far from successful, and why positive policies are neglected. The reason is that government politicians derive personal benefits from using force. The same holds for the members of the military and police forces and secret services. In contrast, there are few proponents of positive anti-terrorist policies. This book argues that appropriate constitutional designs would give the positive approach a better chance.

No general outline of terrorism is provided here – there are many good works doing that. Rather, the book focuses on aspects so far neglected in the literature, as well as on actual anti-terrorist policy. But it does provide an outline of the forms of terrorism in use today and in the past, definitions of terrorism, measurements of terrorist activities, as well as the consequences of terrorism on the economy.

This book is intended for easy reading, despite the (hopefully) precise economic arguments. The text does not use any formalism. A few arguments are illustrated by using simple graphs which are meant to aid understanding. No footnotes or citations (except for verbal quotes) cluster the text. Rather, at the end of each chapter the relevant literature is discussed.

Work on this book has extended over several years. Parts of the material were presented at the Conference on the Economics of Terrorism at the Deutsche Institut fuer Wirtschaftsforschung in Berlin in the spring of 2002, at the 3rd and 4th Corsica Meeting of Law and Economics in Marseille and in Reims, at a conference of the European Public Choice Centre in Rome, and at the Science Centre WZB in Berlin. The bulk of the book was written during a delightful stay as Zijlstra Professorial Fellow at the Netherlands Institute for Advanced Study in the Humanities and Social Sciences (NIAS). So many scholars made comments on the approach to terrorism research presented here that it is impossible to mention them all. I would, however, like to indicate my special debt of gratitude to Roger Congleton, Geoffrey Brennan, Giuseppe Eusepi, Lars Feld, Philipp Jones, Hartmut Kliemt, Kai Konrad, Dennis Mueller, Bill Niskanen, Friedrich Schneider and Ludger Schuknecht.

I am grateful to my co-workers, Dr Matthias Benz, Reto Jegen, Stephan Meier and Dr Alois Stutzer for excellent advice on how to improve the manuscript. Particular thanks are due to Simon Luechinger, with whom I have written several papers on the economics of terrorism and whose insights are reflected in this book. He helped me greatly by making many useful suggestions for clarifying both content and presentation. Anne Simpson of NIAS was kind enough to check the English language. Rosemary Brown carefully and skilfully went through the whole manuscript and greatly improved the style.

PART I

Terrorism and Anti-terrorist Policies

Terrorism exists all over the world and has its origins far back in history. It pursues many different goals, takes many forms and uses many techniques. It therefore makes little sense to seek a strict definition of what terrorism is. Moreover, it greatly depends on one's personal values: 'my freedom fighter is your terrorist'.

Chapter 1 also discusses how the extent and development of terrorist activity over time can be measured by counting the number of violent acts and casualties. However, the relevance of terrorism to the people affected by it should also be taken into account, with possibilities being willingness to pay or subjective well-being studies. Although terrorism can be shown to have severely affected some sectors of the economy (especially tourism and foreign direct investment), it has not proved successful in attaining its goals.

The most prominent anti-terrorist policy is the use of coercive deterrence. Chapter 2 analyses the high costs of fighting terrorism by governmental counter-terrorist measures. They go far beyond the cearly visible budgetary outlays. Moreover, deterrence induces terrorists to substitute their activities, and bolsters their cohesiveness. Not surprisingly, deterrence policy is rarely effective and, in some cases, leads to counterproductive results. The same holds, on the whole, for economic sanctions against 'rogue' countries claimed to harbour terrorists, even when they take the form of smart sanctions or financial boycotts.

Overall, deterrence policy based on applying force is unlikely to be successful and has major costs. It is therefore important to seriously consider alternative anti-terrorist policies going beyond coercion.

1. Terrorism: The Curse of Our Times?

TERRORISM TODAY

This century began with one of the most devastating terrorist acts ever. On September 11, 2001 two passenger aircraft were hijacked by Islamic *al Qaeda* terrorists and deliberately crashed into the twin towers of the World Trade Center in New York, leading to their collapse. The same day another hijacked aircraft crashed into the Pentagon and another crashed in Pennsylvania. These attacks cost a considerable number of lives. The overall death toll amounted to approximately 3000 casualties from more than 90 countries around the world. The event attracted huge media attention. Hundreds of millions of TV viewers witnessed the collapse of the two landmark skyscrapers of New York. It triggered an unprecedented step up in the 'war against terrorism' under the leadership of the United States, supported by a broad coalition of a large number of countries, including all the major powers. As a result, the Taliban government of Afghanistan supporting *al Qaeda* was wiped out. One may rightly say that a new stage in the conflict between terrorists and governments has been reached.

We are today plagued by many other ongoing terrorist activities. It might be useful to mention some of the best-known examples:

- the Basque ETA (*Euzkadi ta Askatasuma*), which regularly assassinates politicians and explodes bombs all over Spain;
- *al Qaeda* exploded bombs in three train stations in Madrid on March 11, 2004, killing around 200 people;
- the IRA (Irish Republican Army) which, since 1969, has undertaken terrorist acts in both Ulster and in Britain, especially in London;
- the PFLP (Popular Front for the Liberation of Palestine), associated to the PLO (Palestine Liberation Organisation), which has undertaken international hijackings and the taking

of hostages. In the same way as *Hamas*, it has more recently
stepped up suicide bombings in Israel to unprecedented levels;

- the PKK (Kurdistan Workers' Party or *Parte Krikaranc
  Kordesian*), which allegedly killed the Swedish prime minister
  Olaf Palme in 1986, but which also has a military wing with
  guerilla fighters active in Turkey, Iran and Iraq;
- the LTTE (Liberation Tigers of Tamil Eelam), whose suicide
  commandos assassinated Prime Minister Rajiv Ghandi of India
  in 1999, a president and a former prime minister of Sri Lanka,
  but who are also involved in more widespread terrorist acts;
- the FARC (*Fuerzas Armadas Revolucionarias de Colombia*),
  which consists of primarily peasants based in specific areas of
  the country and is active in the production and trade of drugs.

This is a rather limited selection of some of the best-known terrorist
organisations presently active. There are virtually hundreds of others.
Terrorism has truly become a threat to peace and prosperity.
Transnational terrorism has become globalised both with respect to
the groups involved and the amount of attention received.

TERRORISM'S LONG HISTORY

Strong terrorist movements all over the world plagued the twentieth
century. In Europe, the 1970s were characterised by left-wing terrorists,
many of whom originated in Marxist, or rather Maoist, intellectual
circles. The RAF (*Rote Armee Fraktion*) emerged in the Federal
Republic of Germany as an offshoot of the student protest movement
sweeping through the universities. The RAF mounted bombing, shooting and arson attacks on government and judicial officials. They also
managed to kill high-ranking business leaders and public officials. Their
failure to force the government to release imprisoned RAF leaders
undermined their support and the group finally disbanded in 1998.

The Italian Red Brigades (*Brigate Rosse*) have a similar origin to
the German RAF. They also unsuccessfully sought the support of the
workers. They killed the (former) Prime Minister Aldo Moro. In the
early 1980s, they were defeated, partly by police action and partly by
those repentant terrorists (*pentiti*) who, in exchange for a generous
remission of sentences, collaborated with the authorities to bring
fellow terrorists to trial.

There were left-wing terrorist groups in other European countries, too. Examples are the *Action Directe* in France or November 17 in Greece.

In Asia, the Japanese Red Army mounted some serious international terrorist attacks, such as the 1972 massacre at Lod Airport, the attacks on the French Embassy in The Hague and the American Embassy in Kuala Lumpur. Today, it operates under the name AIIB (Anti-Imperialist International Brigade), but is rather small and insignificant. More important is the *Aum Shinrikyo* sect, which perpetrated the nerve gas attack on the Tokyo subway in 1995, killing a dozen people and affecting almost 4000 others. The police later found enough sarin gas to kill more than 4 million persons. That particular terrorist group also tried to acquire other biological and nuclear weapons of mass destruction (WMD), such as anthrax, the highly contagious disease known as Q-fever and the deadly Ebola virus.

In South America, there are many terrorist movements. A particularly well-known one is the extreme left-wing Shining Path (*Sendero Luminoso*) in Peru. It has been responsible for savage violence, in particular the assassination of public officials, judges and local community leaders, as well as indiscriminate bombing in Lima. It is estimated to have killed more than 30,000 persons since 1980.

Not even America has been spared terrorist activity in the past. In February 1993, an ad hoc Islamic group called Liberation Army placed a bomb in the garage beneath one of the World Trade towers in the hope of toppling one tower onto the other. This plan did not succeed because the terrorist team made a minor error in their placement of the bomb. Another instance is the 1995 bombing by Timothy McVeigh, associated with the right-wing Christian Patriots, of the Federal Office Building in Oklahoma City, causing the death of 168 persons.

There were instances of terrorism long before the cases mentioned here. The term alludes to the *grande terreur* applied during the French Revolution in 1793–94. One can go back even further, for instance to the assassin sect of Shia Islam, active in Persia and Syria in the twelfth and thirteenth centuries, using daggers to kill their opponents. Well known from history books are the assassination of Czar Alexander II of Russia in 1881 by a bomb planted by anarchists, and the assassination of the Archduke and heir of Austria-Hungary's Emperor Franz Ferdinand of Austria by a Serbian nationalist at Sarajevo in June 1914, sparking off the Great War (World War I). After World War II, terrorism was an integral part of many national liberation struggles in the 1950s and 1960s, such as in Algeria and Cyprus, and became a major international phenomenon.

TYPES OF TERRORISM

The discussion about prominent cases of terrorism presented so far has already made clear that there are many different sorts of terrorism. It is useful to distinguish three types.

Domestic and Transnational Terrorism

There are terrorist groups which, to a large extent, are pursuing their goals, and carrying out actions, but restrict themselves to a particular national territory. The left-wing social revolutionaries, such as the German *Rote Armee Fraktion* or the *Brigate Rosse* are good examples. The same holds for right-wing terrorists, such as those responsible for the bombing in Oklahoma City and some cults, such as the Japanese *Aum Shinrikyo*.

Transnational terrorist groups either want to achieve international goals, such as fighting 'American imperialism' all over the world, or are groups that see a greater chance of attaining their national goals by moving beyond their own frontiers. *Al Qaeda* presents an example of the former, and Palestinian terrorist groups, such as *Hamas*, provide an example of the latter. Among transnational terrorist groups, it is often useful to distinguish between nationalist-separatist groups, such as the IRA, ETA or LTTE, and religious fundamentalist groups of Islamic, Jewish or Christian orientation.

State Sponsored and Religious Terrorism

Some terrorist groups are directly instigated, or at least supported, by states. Such cooperation is especially dangerous when it helps terrorists to acquire chemical, biological or even nuclear weapons of mass destruction. Up to September 11, 2001, many of the most radical terrorists from the Middle East were allegedly actively sponsored by states such as Afghanistan, Iraq, Iran, North Korea, Libya, Syria and Sudan. After the collapse of the German Democratic Republic, it became evident that the *Rote Armee Fraktion* had been actively supported by that regime, and that after the demise of the terrorist group, several of its members had been able to find refuge in that country. Libya was heavily involved in the mid-air bombing of Pan Am flight 103, which crashed in Lockerbie, Scotland, in 1988, claiming the lives of all 259 passengers and crew as well as 11 persons on the ground. There are some indications that state-sponsored terrorism has been decreasing in importance in recent years (Wilkinson, 2000:63). This also means that attacks against 'rogue states' allegedly or actually supporting terrorism promise to have little or no effect.

Clearly, religiously motivated terrorism by radical anti-Western groups has increased considerably. Islamic terrorist groups, such as *al Qaeda* under the leadership of Osama Bin Laden, are in the limelight today, but there are many others who belong to this category, which is not restricted to Islamic terrorist groups. The extremely conservative Christian Patriots were involved in the Oklahoma bombing. There is also a strand of fundamentalist Jewish terrorism. The National Military Organisation (*Irgun Zvai Leumi*) used terrorism to force the British to withdraw from the Palestinian Mandate. Under the command of the man who later became Israeli prime minister and Nobel Peace Prize winner Menachem Begin, *Irgun* blew up a wing of the famous King David Hotel in Jerusalem in 1946, killing 90 people, among them Arabs, Britains and Jews. In 1994, a Jewish follower of Rabbi Kahane and his extreme right wing *Kach* group massacred 29 worshippers in a mosque at Hebron.

Activities Undertaken

Terrorist action can take many different forms. It may, at the one extreme, entail the assassination of a particular government official or politician, such as Anwar Sadat, Indira and Rajiv Ghandi, or Yitzak Rabin. But one should bear in mind that not every murder should be labelled terrorism. The attack must be linked to a particular political goal and the intended effects should go beyond the immediate victim before it can be considered an act of terror.

At the other extreme, terrorists may use weapons of mass destruction; that is, chemical, biological and nuclear means. Biological weapons have been used since 1346, when the Tartars catapulted plague-ridden corpses into the besieged city of Caffa. Terrorists may use biology as a weapon in many different ways. They may spread naturally occurring diseases such as smallpox. As this disease had been eradicated by 1980, people today are 'immunologically naive';

that is, they are as vulnerable to infection as was the American Indian to the poxes of the old world. A study of three US cities showed that an eruption of smallpox would kill at least 1 million people. Although smallpox has not caused any deaths since 1980, and all countries agreed to hand the viruses in their possession to the World Health Organization, WHO, it is thought that some countries are still in possession of this virus. No one can exclude the possibility that terrorists may get hold of the smallpox virus (which is very easy to hide and transport) from one of these states. Equally dangerous, or even more dangerous, are anthrax, botulism, tularaemia, plague and haemorrhagic fever. These diseases cause high death rates and are highly contagious. But there are many other biological and chemical weapons that are nearly as deadly as these, not to mention the huge risk if terrorists were to get hold of nuclear weapons. Up to the present time, such weapons have been used in only a few cases. The use of sarin gas by *Aum Shinrikyo* remains unique. This does not mean that terrorists will not employ them more often and more widely in the future.

Between these two extremes, terrorists have used many different techniques. One means is kidnapping, either to get a ransom (used, for example, by FARC in Colombia) or to liberate followers from imprisonment (which was attempted by the RAF). Another means is hijacking planes or ships (such as the Achille Lauro by the Palestine Liberation Front in 1985), originally for the same purposes, but recently also to serve as flying bombs (as in the attacks of September 11, 2001). Yet other means are armed attacks, the destruction of targets with high symbolic meaning (such as the assassination attempt on Pope John Paul II in the Vatican), or seemingly random attacks on civilians.

WHAT IS TERRORISM?

Efforts to Define Terrorism

It is on purpose that no formal definition of terrorism has been offered so far. It seemed more useful to first present the many different aspects and types of terrorism. One straightforward definition of terrorism is (Harmon, 2000: 1): 'The deliberate and systematic murder, maiming, and menacing of the innocent to inspire fear for political ends'. A frequently used definition by the US State Department (title 22 of the United States Code, section 265f(d)) takes terrorism to be 'premeditated, politically motivated violence perpetrated against noncombatant targets by subnational groups or clandestine agents, usually intended to influence an audience', and the US Department of Defense offers its own definition: 'The unlawful use of – or threatened use of – force or violence against individuals or property to coerce or intimidate governments or societies, often to achieve political, religious, or ideological objectives.'

Many more efforts at defining terrorism may be found in the literature. A scholarly work (Schmid and Jongman, 1988) identifies no less than 109 different definitions of terrorism.

Limits to Defining Terrorism

The definitions presented provide few, if any, useful insights into what terrorism actually is. One of the preeminent scholars of terrorism (Laqueur, 1977: 7) maintains that it is neither possible to provide a definition, nor worthwhile to make the attempt. Terrorism is too complex to grasp with definitions such as those offered so far. In an effort to formally define what terrorism is, two types of error occur: (1) activities that should reasonably count as terrorist acts are excluded; (2) activities that are not terrorist acts are included. A particular definition may easily miss the intended goal of clarifying the issue and may rather lead to confusion.

It is also interesting to note that what is considered 'terrorism' to a large extent depends on political exigencies, and therefore changes according to circumstances and time. Indeed, what one person takes to be a terrorist is seen by another person as a freedom fighter. Hence it is not even given who are the perpetrators and who are the victims.

There are many instances of former terrorists achieving high political positions after some sort of solution has been reached. A complete reversal of the evaluation of who is a freedom fighter and who is a terrorist took place, for instance, in the case of Islamic fighters. Not long ago, the then US President Ronald Reagan said at an official press conference in 1985 (Zambrano, 2001: 9): 'The Mujahedin are the moral equivalent of the Founding Fathers of America'. This was at a time when the US government heavily financed Islamic guerilla to fight against the Soviet invasion of Afghanistan. Today, the situation is totally different, and the Mujahedin are considered to be terrorists.

It has even been argued that certain great historic figures could be considered 'terrorists', at least at some time in their lives. This applies, for instance, to the Roman emperor Augustus, the French *roi de soleil* Louis XIV, the German Chancellor Otto von Bismarck, the British Prime Minister Winston Churchill and the American President Richard Nixon. They all deliberately attacked civilians in an effort to undermine their support for their political leaders, hoping to bring about a change in policy.

Characteristic Elements

This book takes a pragmatic approach to determining what terrorism is, allowing for the interpretation and integration of new phenomena, and provoking further thought on the matter. Moreover, the definition is dependent on the issue in question and can therefore not be generalised.

For practical purposes, the following elements are crucial: the perpetrators:

- use force on civilians;
- act in an unofficial capacity. In particular, they are not part of the national army and do not wear national uniform;
- want to attain political goals;
- intend to have far-reaching effects beyond the immediate victims, particularly through the media.

CAN TERRORISM BE MEASURED?

Basic Issues

As we have seen, terrorism takes many different forms and any definition is questionable. It is therefore extremely difficult to measure. It can even be asked whether it makes sense to place such differing acts involving, for instance, hijacking aircraft for ransom and using nerve gas to spread fear, on the same scale. A major problem is not measuring the occurrence of terrorist events but also evaluating their intensity. What can best be measured is the *number* of terrorist events. But this means that terrorist activities of quite different size are indiscriminately lumped together. The attacks on the World Trade Center would be counted as one (or perhaps two) event(s), and come into the same category as taking one person as a hostage. Such measurements can at best capture general developments, but even then they are useful only if the structure of terrorist events remains more or less unchanged. Thus measuring the number of incidents makes sense if the number of hostage takings and major attacks against buildings by terrorists remains approximately constant. In contrast, if in one year (such as in 2001), a major attack occurred, even if there have been none of that size in preceding or subsequent years, a time series based on the number of acts is of little value.

In order to capture the unequal importance of different terrorist events, other time series measure the *number of casualties*. Some data take the number of persons killed, others (also) consider the number of people injured. In the latter case, the problem arises that being seriously injured, with permanent after-effects (for example, if victims lose their eyesight) differs markedly from being only slightly injured. There can be no strict rule of what to count and what to disregard.

A more adequate way to measure the gravity of terrorist incidents would be to measure the *willingness to pay* (or the marginal utility) for a more peaceful environment of the people affected; that is, being *less* subject to terrorism. Similar techniques could be used to those employed when measuring the willingness to pay for a better natural environment. There are many possible approaches to measuring this subjective willingness to pay (see Frey and Luechinger 2003b), ranging from carefully administered representative surveys to identifying the value attributed by revealed behaviour. The latter method has the great advantage that people are unable to bias their responses as they see fit. When asked about their willingness to pay for lowering the risk of being the target of a terrorist assault, most people are likely to indicate a much higher sum than they are *actually* prepared to spend for that purpose. In contrast, revealed behaviour may consist in analysing how much people actually spend on avoiding terrorism, for instance by moving to another region of the country, by emigrating, or through buying protection designed to safeguard themselves from terrorist attacks (for instance, by hiring private guards). The method has other shortcomings; in particular, it only measures the private benefits from being less subject to terrorism, while disregarding the possibly large external effects. These consist, for instance, of the effect of terrorism on democratic institutions. Individuals' efforts to avoid exposure to threats, and to reduce the harm they suffer if attacked, may also exert positive or negative externalities on other individuals, depending on how the chance of causing harm to one person is influenced by the number of persons similarly exposed.

Willingness to pay approaches are likely to result in higher figures for persons with a high rather than a low income. The distribution of income thus simultaneously affects the measurement of terrorism. But terrorist activities at the same time affect a country's distribution of income, as richer persons tend to emigrate more readily, leaving mostly the poorer people behind in the region or country.

As the experiences from willingness to pay studies for the valuation of the natural environment show, this approach is better suited to identifying restricted micro-economic effects. The method does not work so well, or does not work at all, for the evaluation of macro-economic effects. Thus willingness to pay is, in principle, a good way to measure the subjective importance people attach to rare, and small-scale terrorist events, but it does not provide a solution for measuring the overall importance of terrorism in a country or over a specific time period.

Yet another method of measuring in an aggregate way how much people suffer under terrorism is to analyse the correlation between subjective reported well-being or happiness and the number of terrorist acts. The indicators of happiness are constructed from careful surveys about how satisfied the respondents are with their life as a whole. They have been shown to be a good approximation to individual utility (the indicators are reliable and consistent). These happiness data can then be regressed on a set of explanatory variables reflecting socio-demographic, economic and political conditions, as well as the number of terrorist events. The latter can be broken down to take into account that different types of terrorism may have a different effect on subjective well-being. Using the Euro-Barometer Survey data over the period 1973–98, this approach has been used to estimate the effect of terrorism on the subjective well-being of persons living in French regions much affected by terrorism (the Ile-de-France, including Paris, and Provence-Alpes-Côte d'Azur including Corsica) compared to the rest of France (Frey, Luechinger and Stutzer, 2004). The number of terrorist incidents and the number of people killed are shown to have a statistically significant and sizeable effect on reported life satisfaction. For 25 terrorist acts (which corresponds to the average number of terrorist acts per year in France in the period studied), on average, satisfaction with life falls by 0.07 units on the four-point scale. This approach also allows us to calculate the increase in houshold income necessary to offset the consequences of terrorism according to the individuals' own evaluation. An increase of nine terrorist acts per year requires a compensation of 1200 euros per year (about 6 per cent of average income). If the number of persons killed by terrorists rises by 2.5 per year, the average French person requires an increase in household income of 830 euros (about 4 per cent) as a compensation to feel equally well off. These figures also suggest how much French people would be willing to pay for a *decrease* in terrorism. Similar magnitudes for compensations have been identified on labour and housing markets for individuals living in American states, with the highest rate of violent crime, compared with regions with less crime (see Blomquist, Berger and Hoehn, 1988). Another study (Hess, 2003) calculates that, on average, individuals who live in a country that has experienced some conflict in the 1960–92 period would permanently give up approximately 8 per cent of their current consumption level in order to live in a purely peaceful world. The study on the effect of terrorism on self-reported well-being is consistent with these results. However, it makes a more realistic comparison than the study by Hess, as it makes a comparison of the welfare level between persons living in regions of France with different amounts of terrorism, not with the ideal and unrealistic condition of perfect peace. Irrespective of what method is employed to measure the extent and importance of terrorism, the most important consideration must be for what purpose the measurement is undertaken. As will be shown in the next section, even rather crude measures of terrorist activity are useful for answering specific questions, for instance how terrorism affects tourism or foreign direct investment.

There is yet another basic problem connected with the measurement of terrorism. Only those terrorist events reflected in official statistics and in the media can be counted. Reliance on official statistics is often mistaken, because the authorities either do not know themselves or deliberately bias their reporting. The media only pick up some terrorist events, mostly those occurring in the larger cities or the capital of a country where the foreign journalists tend to reside. Terrorist action taking place in remote rural areas is rarely, if ever, reported in the media.

Data Series

The US State Department issues a series covering the number of terrorist events, number of persons killed and injured. It employs the official US definition of terrorism reproduced earlier. Table 1.1 provides the data for the period 1977–2000.

The number of terrorist events recorded in this statistic varies considerably from 274 to 665. No clear trend is visible. At its height, more than 600 attacks took place in the years 1985–88 and since then there

Table 1.1   Transnational terrorism, 1977–2000; number of events, persons killed and injured

Year	Number of events	Deaths	Wounded
1977	419	230	404
1978	530	435	629
1979	434	697	542
1980	499	507	1062
1981	489	168	804
1982	487	128	755
1983	497	637	1267
1984	565	312	967
1985	635	825	1217
1986	612	604	1717
1987	665	612	2272
1988	605	407	1131
1989	375	193	397
1990	437	200	675
1991	565	102	233
1992	363	93	636
1993	431	109	1393
1994	322	314	663
1995	440	163	6291
1996	296	314	2652
1997	304	211	693
1998	274	741	5952
1999	395	233	706
2000	426	405	791

Source: US State Department, *Patterns of Global Terrorism* (various years) and Sandler and Enders (2002), Table 1.

has been a decline. This finding contrasts with the general notion that terrorism has become an ever increasing threat.

The number of people killed in terrorist attacks also varies considerably, from 825 in 1985 to 93 in 1992. But again, no clear trend is visible. The same applies to the number of persons injured. It varies even more strongly from 233 in 1991 to 6291 in 1995. The data series is greatly influenced by spectacular events, such as the simultaneous bombing of the American embassies in Kenya and Tanzania in 1998, causing a total of 291 deaths and 5000 injured.

Figure 1.1 shows the annual time series for the number of incidents and the number of persons killed in the period 1977–2000.

Altogether, the series on transnational terrorism compiled by the US Department of State seems to cover only a rather restricted part of overall terrorist activities throughout the world. The number of persons killed through terrorist activities is rather small in comparison with, for example, those killed in traffic accidents – 40,000 people are killed each year in traffic accidents in the United States alone. Another data series has been constructed by Mickolus (1982), and

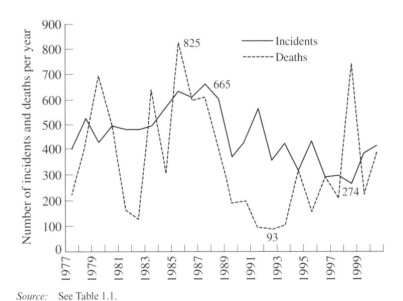

Source: See Table 1.1.

Figure 1.1   Transitional terrorism, 1977–2000; number of events and persons killed

has recently been extended by Fleming (2001) and Sandler and Enders (2002). It is called ITERATE, *International Terrorism: Attributes of Terrorist Events.* It relies solely on newspaper reports and picks up *newsworthy* transnational terrorist events.

A common observation made by many scholars studying terrorism is that, while the level of transnational terrorist incidents has been declining since the early or mid-1990s, the number of persons killed and injured has not been reduced as much. Terrorism has become increasingly lethal. According to Enders and Sandler (2000), in recent years an attack is about 17 percentage points more likely to result in casualties than in the 1970s. This increased lethality has been attributed to the increasing proportion of fundamentalist terrorist groups seeking mass casualties of innocent people to make their cause more widely known. In contrast, the leftist-based and nationalist terrorists want to instigate a revolution and aim at winning the hearts of the people. They therefore avoid killing or maiming innocent people not directly connected with the existing political and economic regime.

Using spectral analysis on the quarterly series of various terrorist activities (ITERATE data), a number of cycles have been identified (Enders and Sandler, 2002). It has been found that logistically complicated incidents, such as large-scale suicide car bombings, the hijacking of aircraft and assassinations have a longer duration than less sophisticated events.

Several reasons have been adduced as to why terrorist activity develops in cycles rather than as a continuous movement in one direction:

- demonstration and imitation effects act as propagators;
- economies of scale in planning terrorist incidents lower the cost for a restricted period of time;
- after a terrorist act, there is a public outcry, inducing the authorities in all possible target countries to take strong action which, again for a restricted period of time, reduces transnational terrorist activity. This 'attack–counterattack cycle' (Enders and Sandler, 1999) produces fluctuations.

CONSEQUENCES OF TERRORISM ON THE ECONOMY

Over the last few years, scholars have analysed the effects terrorist acts have on various aspects of the economy.

Tourism

Terrorists have often used tourists as targets, because they are easy to attack and attract a lot of attention from the media. The effect on the choice of tourist location is considerable. The expected cost of a holiday in a country under threat of terrorist attacks is higher than for vacation in an alternative location without the threat of terrorism. The host country is therefore substantially negatively affected by terrorist attacks. At the same time, the resonance in the media is huge. The bombing, shooting and kidnapping of tourists often has a highly positive expected net benefit to terrorists and is therefore frequently undertaken. An example is the Luxor massacre, in which the terrorists of the Islamic Group shot dead 58 foreign tourists visiting the temple of Queen Hatshepsut in the Valley of the Queens in 1997. Another example is the bombing of a disco in Bali in 2002, costing the lives of almost 200 tourists, mostly Australians.

Careful econometric analyses, applying advanced time series (vector auto-regression VAR) methods and the ITERATE terrorism data (for example, Enders, Parise and Sandler, 1992), have been used to study the relationship between terrorism and tourism. The causal direction was found to run from terrorism to tourism. For Spain, in which not only the Basque ETA, but also other left-wing groups (such as the CAA, GRAPO) have committed terrorist acts, it has been estimated that a typical terrorist incident scares away over 140,000 tourists when all the monthly impacts are combined. Similar results have been found for other tourist destinations, such as Greece, Italy, Austria, Turkey and Israel. Terrorism thus has a substantial effect on tourism. It is transitory but, compared with a situation in which no, or fewer, terrorist acts are committed, the loss of income for the host country is huge. The relevant comparison is not the number of tourists before the event, because without the event the number of tourists would most likely have risen.

Foreign Direct Investment

The effect of terrorism on foreign firms investing money into real foreign assets is also considerable. Terrorists can quite easily attack and damage foreign owned firms, seriously disrupting their activities. They may even be supported, or at least not hindered, by domestic competitors for goods, services and labour. As the foreigners have a large choice of countries to invest in, even quite mild terrorist activities tend to strongly affect the inflow of capital to a terror-stricken country.

This has indeed been found to be the case for Spain and Greece, again using the VAR methodology and the ITERATE quarterly terrorism data (Enders and Sandler, 1996). In Spain, terrorism is estimated to have reduced annual direct foreign investment inflow by 13.5 per cent on average for the period 1968–91. This translates into a decline in real direct foreign investment of almost 500 million dollars, or 7.6 per cent of annual gross fixed capital formation. As direct foreign investment is an important source of saving, investment and economic growth are negatively affected. Moreover, the transfer of technological know-how into the country was reduced, again putting a dampener on growth.

In the same period of time, Greece was plagued by two major terrorist organisations, the 17 November and the Revolutionary Popular Struggle. Both are extreme left-wing movements. The reduction of direct foreign investment was estimated to be, on average, 11.9 per cent annually. This translates into a loss amounting to almost 400 million dollars, or 34.8 per cent of annual gross fixed capital formation. These economic costs are substantial.

Foreign Trade

Using an extended gravity model containing the conventional determinants and, in addition, the extent of terrorist activity in a country, it has been estimated that doubling the extent of terrorist attacks reduces the bilateral trade flows by 6 per cent (Nitsch and Schumacher, 2004).

Stock Market

Between 1998 and 1999, the Basque ETA (*Euzkadi ta Askatasuna*) declared a cease-fire. This can be taken to be a natural experiment to estimate the cost of the terrorist conflict in terms of its effect on the stock value of a sample of Basque and non-Basque firms. If the terrorist conflict was perceived to have a negative effect on the Basque economy, stocks of firms with a significant part of their business activity in the Basque country should exhibit a positive relative performance when the truce began, and a negative relative performance when the truce ended. Basque stocks did indeed outperform non-Basque stocks as the truce became credible. At the end of the cease-fire, Basque stocks showed a negative performance relative to non-Basque stocks (Abadie and Gardeazabal, 2003).

Urban Economy

Terrorism may influence the relative advantage of living in a city compared with living in the country. Violence may affect urbanisation by making it possible to exploit the positive economies of scale of defending a city. At the same time, the high population density makes cities an attractive target for terrorists. Finally, violence and terrorism raise transport costs. They can be substituted by closer physical vicinity. The last two influences are most relevant for modern terrorism, but they point in opposite directions. An analysis of the population development of London, Jerusalem, Tel Aviv and Haifa, as a reaction to the various types and intensity of terrorism, does not provide a clear answer as to how terrorist acts promote or hinder urbanisation (Glaeser and Shapiro, 2001).

Various studies have estimated the economic effects of the terrorist attacks on September 11, 2001. The direct costs consist of the destruction of real investment and human capital. The collapse of the twin towers destroyed 13 million square feet of real estate, and 30 per cent of superior office space in downtown New York. But this accounts for only 4 per cent of the total office space situated in Manhattan. One estimate of the real and human capital costs ranges from 25 to 60 billion dollars (Becker and Murphy, 2001b). Another study considers the loss of human capital to be 40 billion dollars, and the property loss at between 10 and 13 billion dollars (Navarro and Spencer, 2001). Yet another estimate of the total direct loss is 21.4 billion dollars (International Monetary Fund, 2001). Looking at the destruction relative to the overall US productive capacity indicates that the damage was minor (Brauer, 2002). The estimates of between 10 and 60 billion dollars worth of damage by the attacks of

September 11, 2001 is relatively small compared with the American GNP of 10 trillion dollars.

However, the indirect costs may be substantial. They consist of the induced cost of doing business, for instance longer waiting times at airports, higher friction and transactions costs in international trade, and the cost of the military and civilian resources used to fight terrorism. To achieve a significant reduction in the probability of falling prey to a terrorist attack is certainly expensive. The share of the economic potential able to be used for consumption today and in the future is significantly reduced. But it is impossible to attach any serious figure to these factors. This is particularly so if the effects outside the United States are also taken into account. Based on a computable general equilibrium model (Walkenhorst and Dihel, 2002), it has been estimated that the indirect cost of increased economic friction in international trade is larger for other regions of the world than for North America.

National Income

Estimating the effect of terrorism on the economy is faced with the problem of how the economy would have developed if there had been less terrorism, or no terrorism at all. To construct a counterfactual is not easy. An interesting attempt has been made for the Basque country where a 'synthetic' control region was created, made up of other Spanish regions, but in many ways resembling the relevant economic characteristics of the Basque country before the onset of political terrorism in the 1970s. The subsequent economic development of this counterfactual synthetic region was compared with the actual experience of the Basque country. It is estimated that, after the outbreak of terrorism, the per capita GDP in the Basque country fell by about 10 percentage points relative to the control region. This gap tends to widen when terrorist activities are on the increase (Abadie and Gardeazabal, 2003).

These six instances of the effects of terrorist actions on the economy do not attempt to calculate the overall costs of terrorism. As has been argued, such costs can only be appropriately measured by evaluating the willingness to pay of individuals to live in an environment with less or no terrorism. It certainly does not suffice to consider the cost of the anti-terrorist policy. Such costs may be, and hopefully are, much lower than the loss of utility experienced by individuals subject to terrorism.

This applies even more fully to the cost of protection against terrorist acts. For instance, the information that the Spanish authorities spent about 350 million dollars to protect the Olympic Games in Barcelona in 1992 (Harmon, 2000: 69) is of quite limited relevance. More relevant are the repurcussions on terrorism risk insurance. The threats of terrorism have led to insurance for this risk being unavailable, or at least being more costly in terms of the premiums to be paid.

It should be firmly kept in mind that the direct costs imposed by terrorists are often not high. More relevant are the costs generated by the reactions to the terrorist attacks. It is therefore important to analyse carefully how the governments in the countries affected respond to terrorism. As will be argued in the next chapter, these reaction costs are particularly high when the response focuses mainly or even exclusively on deterrence.

HAS TERRORISM BEEN SUCCESSFUL?

Interestingly enough, there is a broad consensus among leading scholars in the field that terrorism – despite media attention – has been quite *unsuccessful*. To quote recent statements of leading experts: 'modern terrorism . . . has been remarkably unsuccessful in gaining strategic objectives' (Wilkinson, 2000: 13); and 'the political effectiveness of terrorism is generally short-term and limited in scope' (Crenshaw, 2001: 15606). The same view is shared by the originator of the economic study of terrorism, Tom Schelling: 'Acts of terrorism never appear to accomplish anything politically significant . . . terrorism has proved to be a remarkably ineffectual means to achieve anything' (Schelling, 1991: 20–21).

These scholars may well be right. However, can these conclusions be accepted at face value? In order to be able to give a scientifically respectable answer to the question of whether terrorism has been successful, it is necessary to focus on two more basic questions:

1. *What is meant by 'successful?'* Depending on the many different goals terrorists may have, a seemingly unsuccessful action may in fact be successful. For instance, if the only goal of a terrorist was to gain media attention, it is irrelevant whether any other goal is reached. This means that the *utility function* or *motivational structure* of the terrorists needs to be analysed.

2. *'Successful compared to what?'* Terrorists may have political influence, but other actions, such as peaceful political campaigning, may achieve more. This means that a *comparative stance* has to be taken.

These two questions will be the focus of the following chapters. In particular, we will see that the same questions arise when the effects of anti-terror policies are considered. But, whatever the outcome of that analysis, one thing has become clear in this chapter: terrorism is dangerous and involves high costs to all participants, be they the targets or the terrorists. Small groups of terrorists with low costs can impose huge costs on others.

SUGGESTED FURTHER READING

There are many excellent and detailed accounts of terrorism today and in history. Particularly useful general works are:

Wilkinson, Paul (2000). *Terrorism Versus Democracy: The Liberal State Response.* London: Frank Cass.
Harmon, Christopher C. (2000). *Terrorism Today*. London: Frank Cass.
Hoffman, Bruce (1998). *Inside Terrorism*. New York: Columbia University Press.
Wieviorka, Michel (1993). *The Making of Terrorism*. Chicago and London: University of Chicago Press.

While all these books consider the history of terrorism, that particular aspect is at the centre of the work by Parry:

Parry, Albert (1976). *Terrorism. From Robespierre to Arafat*. New York: Vanguard Press.

The behaviour of the assassin terrorist sect is discussed and put into theoretical perspective by Konrad:

Konrad, Kai A. (2002). 'Terrorism and the State'. WZB, Social Science Research Center Berlin discussion papers.

All these works refer to the large amount of further literature available. A concise summary is provided in the article by Crenshaw.

Crenshaw, Martha (2001). 'Terrorism'. In Neil J. Smelser and Paul B. Baltes (eds), *International Encyclopedia of the Social and Behavioral Sciences*, Vol. 23. Amsterdam: Pergamon; pp. 15604–06.

The terrorist scene in Europe is well treated in essays collected by the following:

Schmid, Alex P. and Ronald D. Crelinsten (eds) (1993). *Western Responses to Terrorism*. London: Frank Cass.

An extensive discussion of types of terrorism is presented in:

Hudson, Rex A. (1999). *The Sociology and Psychology of Terrorism. Who Becomes a Terrorist and Why?* Washington, DC: Federal Research Division, Library of Congress [Internet: http://www.fas.org/irp/frd.html].
Lesser, Ian O., Bruce Hoffman, John Arquilla, David F. Ronfeldt, Michele Zanini and Brian Michael Jensen (1999). *Countering the New Terrorism*. Santa Monica, CA: Rand Corporation.

The danger arising from state-sponsored terrorism is, for instance, analysed in:

Quillen, Chris (2000). 'State-sponsored WMD Terrorism: A Growing Threat?' Mimeo, Terrorism Research Center [Internet: www.terrorism.com].

A thorough discussion of the definitional aspects of terrorism is provided in:

Schmid, Alex P. and Albert J. Jongman (1988). *Political Terrorism: A New Guide to Actors, Authors, Concepts, Data Bases, Theories, and Literature*. New Brunswick, NJ: Transaction Books.
Stern, Jessica (1999). *The Ultimate Terrorists*. Cambridge, MA and London: Harvard University Press.

There is a huge literature on the evaluation of the value of environmental quality. The most prominent approach today is 'contingent valuation'. It is discussed in:

Diamond, Peter A. and Jerry A. Hausman (1994). 'Contingent Valuation: Is Some Number Better than No Number?' *Journal of Economic Perspectives* **8** (4): 45–64.

The economics of happiness is treated in:

Frey, Bruno S. and Alois Stutzer (2002). *Happiness and Economics. How the Economy and Institutions Affect Human Well-being*. Princeton, NJ: Princeton University Press.

A survey on the various approaches to measuring terrorism and the use of subjective well-being data to estimate the cost of terrorism is given in:

Frey, Bruno S. and Simon Luechinger (2003). 'Measuring Terrorism'. IEW Working Paper No. 171, University of Zurich.
Frey, Bruno S., Simon Luechinger and Alois Stutzer (2004). 'Valuing Public Goods: The Life Satisfaction Approach'. IEW Working Paper No. 184, University of Zurich.

The discussion of the data follows the excellent presentation in:

Sandler, Todd and Walter Enders (2004). 'An Economic Perspective on Transnational Terrorism'. *European Journal of Political Economy*, forthcoming.

The *International Terrorism: Attributes of Terrorist Events* data are due to:

Mickolus, Edward F. (1982). *International Terrorism: Attributes of Terrorist Events 1968–1977. (ITERATE 2)*. Ann Arbor, MI: Inter-University Consortium for Political and Social Research.

They have been updated by the following:

Mickolus, Edward F., Todd Sandler, Jean M. Murdock and Peter Fleming (1989). *International Terrorism: Attributes of Terrorist Events, 1978–1987. (ITERATE 3)*. Dunn Loring, VA: Vinyard Software.
Mickolus, Edward F., Todd Sandler, Jean M. Murdock and Peter Fleming (1993). *International Terrorism: Attributes of Terrorist Events, 1988–1991. (ITERATE 4)*. Dunn Loring, VA: Vinyard Software.
Fleming, Peter (2001). 'International Terrorism: Attributes of Terrorist Events 1992–1998'. (ITERATE 5 update). Mimeo.

Cycles in terrorist activity are discussed in:

Hoffman, Bruce (1998). *Inside Terrorism*. New York: Columbia University Press.
Lesser, Ian O., Bruce Hoffman, John Arquilla, David F. Ronfeldt, Michele Zanini and Brian Michael Jensen (1999). *Countering the New Terrorism*. Santa Monica, CA: Rand Corporation.

Central contributions are from:

Enders, Walter, Gerald F. Parise and Todd Sandler (1992). 'A Time-series Analysis of Transnational Terrorism: Trends and Cycles'. *Defence Economics* **3** (4): 305–20.
Enders, Walter and Todd Sandler (2002). 'Patterns of Transnational Terrorism, 1970–99: Alternative Time Series Estimates'. *International Studies Quarterly* **46**: 145–65.

The effects of terrorism on tourism have been studied, for instance, by the following:

Enders, Walter and Todd Sandler (1991). 'Causality Between Transnational Terrorism and Tourism: The Case of Spain'. *Terrorism* **14**: 49–58.
Enders, Walter, Todd Sandler and Gerald F. Parise (1992). 'An Econometric Analysis of the Impact of Terrorism on Tourism'. *Kyklos* **45** (4): 531–54.
Pizam, Abraham and Ginger Smith (2000). 'Tourism and Terrorism: A Quantitative Analysis of Major Terrorist Acts and their Impact on Tourism Destinations'. *Tourism Economics* **6** (2): 123–38.
Drakos, Konstantinos and Ali M. Kutan (2003). 'Regional Effects of Terrorism on Tourism in Three Mediterranean Countries'. *Journal of Conflict Resolution* **47**(5): 621–641.

The study on the effect of terrorism on foreign direct investment in Spain and Greece is due to:

Enders, Walter and Todd Sandler (1996). 'Terrorism and Foreign Direct Investment in Spain and Greece'. *Kyklos* **49** (3): 331–52.

The effect on foreign trade has been estimated in:

Nitsch, Volker and Dieter Schumacher (2004). 'Terrorism and International Trade: An Empirical Investigation'. *European Journal of Political Economy*, forthcoming.

The impact of terrorism on the stock market and on national income has been analysed in the case of the Basque country by the following:

Abadie, Alberto and Javier Gardeazabal (2003). 'The Economic Costs of Conflict: A Case Study for the Basque Country'. *American Economic Review* **93** (1): 113–32.

How terrorism and urbanisation interact has been studied in:

Glaeser, Edward L. and Jesse M. Shapiro (2001). 'Cities and Warfare: The Impact of Terrorism on Urban Form'. *Journal of Urban Economics* **51**: 205–24.

The direct and indirect economic costs of September 11, 2001 have been estimated in:

Becker, Gary S. and Kevin Murphy (2001). 'Prosperity Will Rise Out of the Ashes'. *Wall Street Journal*, 29 October 2001.
International Monetary Fund (2001). 'How Has September 11 Influenced the Global Economy?' *World Economic Outlook*, Chapter 11.
Navarro, Peter and Aron Spencer (2001). 'September 2001: Assessing the Costs of Terrorism'. *Milken Institute Review* **2**: 16–31.

Congleton, Roger D. (2002). 'Terrorism, Interest-group Politics, and Public Policy: Curtailing Criminal Modes of Political Speech'. *Independent Review* **7** (1): 47–67.

The effects of terrorism threats on insurance availability and premiums are the subject of:

Brown, Jeffrey R., Randall S. Krozner and Brian H. Jenn (2002). 'Federal Terrorism Risk Insurance'. *National Tax Journal*, **55** (3): 647–657.

2. Using Deterrence Against Terrorism

PREDOMINANCE OF COERCIVE ANTI-TERROR POLICY

Governments may react to terrorism in two basic ways:

1. *Using the 'stick'*: This coercive approach works with using negative sanctions, mostly by employing military and police enforcement. Persons undertaking terrorist acts are severely punished either by killing them or by putting them in prison, possibly after torturing them. This response is based on immediate and strong retribution and addresses the most urgent problems created by a terrorist attack. The response is 're-active' in so far as it is incident-related, dealing with terrorist attacks that have already taken place.

2. *Using the 'carrot'*: Actual and potential terrorists are given positive incentives to desist from their violent activities by providing them with superior alternatives, but also by reducing the benefits they derive from terrorist acts. This approach seeks to address the root causes of terrorism. It considers reforms addressing the grievances of the terrorists and is directed at prevention or long-term reform. It is 'pro-active', in so far as it identifies newly emerging political conflicts possibly leading to terrorism.

The two basic types of approach suggest different policies open to governments and imply different benefits and costs, both to the terrorists and to the governments undertaking the policies. A deterrent response, involving the use of military force, is likely to be accompanied by higher budgetary costs. A policy based on offering terrorists alternatives may seem to be cheap in comparison, but may create political costs to the government, as the people may consider it a 'cowardly' response. However, a coercive response may also have its political costs, in particular when it proves impossible to provide quick successes.

The prevailing response to terrorist attacks has been coercive counter-terrorism using military and police forces. This holds, in particular, for today's only global power, the United States, but also for many other nations, such as Britain in the past and Israel in the present. The US armed forces, originally designed for military war against another military power (the Soviet Union and its satellites), is being transformed into an instrument to fight the 'war against terrorism', as proclaimed by President Bush in the wake of the attacks of September 11, 2001.

Deterrence is not necessarily the same as using brute force. Deterrence involves the *threat* of damage to an adversary. It would be most successful if it were possible not to actually carry it out. Deterrence gives the opponent, in this case the terrorist group, the possibility to choose whether to desist from future violent action, or to pursue its violent activities. In the latter case, it is sanctioned by heavy costs. But the difference between deterrence and brute force tends to vanish, because deterrence is only credible and therefore effective if it is regularly used. Indeed, the idea of a deterrent strategy is to impose so great a cost when it is exercised that the terrorists find the expected value of pursuing their course of action to be disadvantageous to them.

An example of the use of force in terrorist policy is President Reagan's response to the hostage taking of Americans in their embassy in Teheran in 1981 when he promised 'swift and effective retribution'. When it turned out that Libya was involved in the bombing of a disco in Berlin frequented by American soldiers, 'Operation El Dorado Canyon' was started in April 1986. President Gaddafi's home and headquarters were bombed in a (failed) assassination attempt.

Many governments see the use of military and police forces as the only way of effectively countering terrorism. They abhor what they consider to be 'concessions' to terrorists and rely on threats of punishment. The most effective negative sanctions are seen in military strikes, aggressive activity (including kidnapping and killing) aimed at individuals known to be, or suspected of being terrorists, or against persons and nations supporting and harbouring terrorists. Overt and covert military and paramilitary action is also thought advisable to pre-empt and prevent actions by terrorist groups, as well as to target countries suspected of hosting or tolerating terrorists.

The literature on terrorism has predominantly dealt with deterrence. Much has been written on the use of military and economic sanctions against individual terrorists and their supporters, and even more on its use against nations supposed to support or harbour terrorists. In contrast, little attention has been devoted to the role of positive sanctions in shaping the behaviour of terrorists and countries.

The coercive approach is the subject of the present chapter. The anti-terror policies based on providing positive incentives form the core of the later parts of this book.

CONSEQUENCES OF DETERRENCE

The use of negative sanctions to deter actual and potential terrorists has both advantages and disadvantages for the country undertaking them. They will each be discussed in turn.

Benefits

The potential benefits to the country undertaking an anti-terrorist policy built on using force, lies in the expected high costs imposed on terrorists. It is predicted that they will react by desisting from the violent activities in order to avoid these negative consequences. Deterrence is also thought to work against 'rogue states' harbouring terrorists – but this can only be effective if the terrorists solely depend on a particular country or countries which can be attacked, not when the terrorists are footloose. But many terrorist organisations have a flexible network structure and therefore do not depend on particular countries. In that case, using force against particular states cannot reach the goal of eradicating terrorism.

The advantages of undertaking a deterrence policy are hard to isolate and to measure, particularly because of possible indirect and long-term effects on the behaviour of potential and actual terrorists. The basic problem is to identify how much worse off (if at all) the victims of terrorism would have been if no deterrence policy had been undertaken. Such a counterfactual situation is difficult to construct, especially as long-run and macro-economic and macro-societal effects have to be taken into account.

Costs

Some of the costs of undertaking a deterrence policy are readily apparent and measurable. It is useful to distinguish costs falling directly on the initiator of the deterrence policy from those induced in response by the terrorists, as well as more general costs.

Direct costs for the country undertaking the deterrence policy

Budgetary costs   There are substantial costs involved in the prevention of a terrorist attack, such as border controls, being prepared for an emergency, scientific research on the consequences of terrorist attacks (in particular with respect to chemical, biological and nuclear attacks by terrorists) and the collection and interpretation of information undertaken by intelligence agencies. The more aggressive part of the deterrence policy relies on the military and police forces and the various secret services. The total number of employees and the actual budget is hard to identify, because much of it is not public knowledge. In the United States, the Department of Homeland Security (established in 2002) alone is expected to carry out anti-terrorist measures using 169,000 employees (most of them in the Border and Transportation Security section) and an annual budget of 37 billion dollars. But there are many other agencies involved in the 'war against terrorism', above all the four branches of the armed forces.

The overall budgetary costs of anti-terrorist policy are certainly substantial. But it must, of course, be taken into consideration that not all expenditures for defence should be attributed to deterrence policy. Some parts serve different purposes, such as that of dissuading the armed forces of other nations from attacking.

Political costs   A deterrence policy may produce domestic policy costs. The question is to what extent, for how long, and in what ways the citizens are prepared to support such a policy. In the case of the United States, one of the major proponents of deterrence policy, it seems that air strikes are seen by the US public and many decision makers as a suitable means of intervening at low cost, especially in terms of prospective American casualties. In that case, the political costs of deterrence policy are zero, or even negative from the point of view of the government. But the political costs become visible when the mostly indirect costs on the economy, in the form of budget deficits and commitment of labour to these purposes, are on the increase.

Another type of political cost can arise from international coalition partners, who may not fully support, or perhaps even oppose, the particular deterrence policy undertaken. This can lead to strains and conflicts, which certainly need to be counted among the costs.

Costs in terms of reduced human and political rights Deterrence policy involving the use of force always runs the risk of resorting to repressive means. In the name of the 'war on terrorism', civil liberties are undermined or completely suppressed:

- surveillance of the population as a whole, and in particular of certain groups, is intensified;
- some groups and actions are found guilty by association, for instance because of 'ethnic profiling', rather than because of having undertaken any unlawful activity;
- the fundamental constitutional principle of 'due process' is redefined and for some persons abolished; and
- oversight on the part of parliament or courts is resisted or even banned.

This concern has been frequently discussed in connection with the anti-terrorist policy undertaken in the United States after September 11, 2001, especially by the 'Patriot Act' pushed through Congress shortly after this traumatic event. For the citizens concerned, these reductions in human and political rights form part of the costs of deterrence policy. Such a response plays right into the hands of the terrorists and, if it goes too far, becomes totally counter-productive.

Costs of this type do not only arise domestically, but also internationally. If a country undertaking a deterrence policy violates international agreements and norms, a cumulative worsening of the relationships between countries may take place. A pertinent example would be terrorists attacking an embassy. If the nation affected responds by also violating diplomatic immunity, everybody is worse off. The rules agreed on, and developed over centuries of diplomatic relations, are then destroyed. Undermining the public good of international law must be counted among the most important costs of deterrence policy.

Exploitation by governments   The main goal of government politicians is to remain in power. In order to survive in a democracy, they need to win the next elections. In authoritarian or dictatorial political systems, the governments are usually able to rig the 'elections', sometimes to the ridiculous extent of receiving 99.9 per cent of the votes. But they must take precautions against being toppled by other politicians, a popular movement, or a revolution. In order to ensure that they remain in power, all governments are tempted by the opportunity of exploiting terrorist attacks to their own advantage.

There have been suggestions from many sides (for instance Falk, 2003; Congleton, 2002) that President Bush skilfully used the terrorist attacks of September 11, 2001 by exploiting the 'rally around the flag' effect regularly following national disasters. He was able to convince the voters that he incorporates the will of the nation, and that not supporting him (and his party) comes close to being anti-American. As a result, the strong version of deterrence policy undertaken by his administration was accepted as the only conceivable response to the terrorist attacks. This policy paid off. In the mid-term elections in the autumn of 2002, President Bush gained a majority in both houses of the Congress. This is noteworthy, as the President's party normally loses seats at mid-term elections.

In a well-functioning democracy, in which the checks and balances work well, there is nothing to be said against such dealings. They are part of the process of political competition. The preferences of the population are only violated if political competition is restricted by the government, for instance by reducing human and political rights (see above), or if the activities of the competing parties and politicians are in some way hampered. Democracy can also be undermined by a deterrence policy, if deviating views are not tolerated because they are claimed to help the terrorist cause. The coercive nature of deterrence policy tends to favour such violations of political rights more than would be the case with an anti-terrorist policy based on positive incentives. Authoritarian and dictatorial governments often exploit terrorist activities to suppress their own people. In the name of the fight against terrorism, any opposition to the government is declared illegal. Freedom of the press is curtailed. In each case, the government claims that the terrorist cause is helped. A deterrence policy is thus used to strengthen the grip over the people. Such anti-democratic measures are often to be found in countries concentrated on their military fight against terrorism. One example is Russia. By joining the alliance against terrorism formed by the United States, the Russian government is now able to suppress human and political rights in order to fight the rebellion in Chechenya, without having to fear any resistance or even critique by the US. The costs in terms of loss of freedom and political sovereignty of individuals have to be considered when assessing deterrence policy.

Increased vulnerability A coercion-oriented response to terrorism tends to raise the degree of centralisation in the polity and economy. This makes the respective country more attractive as a target. The increased vulnerability constitutes a cost to be reckoned with (see the extensive discussion of this issue in Chapter 5).

Effects due to terrorists' response to deterrence policy

Induced substitution Full deterrence is impossible, as it would imply infinite costs. No country, not even one having extensive surveillance and punishing power, is able to thwart all conceivable future terrorist activity. This is impossible with existing terrorist threats, and even more so with regard to as yet unknown future terrorist actions. Experience has shown that terrorists are capable of innovative responses to deterrence policy. They do not only seek new ways of achieving their goals, but they quickly find substitutes for those targets that are impossible or too costly to protect. Examples are the bombing of a disco in Bali, and the hijacking of a theatre in Moscow in autumn 2002, both of which cost hundreds of lives, but which happened when the post-September 11 deterrence policy was in full swing. The costs are further increased if the terrorists turn their attention from less harmful to more harmful objectives, resulting in higher casualties and damage.

Increased visibility A deterrence policy must necessarily identify the adversary, but this in turn focuses media attention on their existence and cause. The terrorists thereby achieve one of their major objectives. This is a cost attributable to deterrence response (but may possibly also apply to some other anti-terrorist policies). This aspect is the subject of Chapter 7.

Increased terrorists' cohesiveness and influence A coercive response reinforces the differences between the population at large and the activists undertaking terrorist attacks. At the same time, it exacerbates nationalism and xenophobia in the countries more or less associated with the terrorists. The terrorists are thereby strengthened, resulting in higher costs for the country undertaking the deterrence policy. An example is provided by the Israeli experience with *Hezbollah* and the Palestine Liberation Organisation (PLO) in Lebanon. The strikes of the Israeli army helped PLO recruitment by demonstrating PLO's commitment to the struggle against Israel. Moreover, the Palestinian terrorist organisations received increased support from sympathetic local and international sponsors. The Lebanese *Hezbollah* was able to attract more money from abroad and provoked a nationalist backlash. This in turn strengthened *Hezbollah*'s position in the Lebanese community.

Costs of failed delivery   A coercive response claims to be able to deliver a clear victory over the terrorists. If the coercer is not successful, deterrence policy tends to become unpopular in the country undertaking it. A natural reaction by the government is to use even more force against the terrorists. If this does not result in resounding success, resistance to the deterrence policy may increase further. The terrorists may well be able to predict this sequence of events, and their determination may increase when they sense that the coercive policy is unsustainable because of the high economic and political costs involved.

General costs

Deterrence is based on a negative approach: terrorists are threatened with punishment if they continue their activities. Coercive action is answered by coercive action. Such interaction tends to degenerate into a *negative sum game* between the parties involved, making each of them worse off: both the country engaging in the coercive response and the terrorists lose. Any war, including the proclaimed 'war against terrorism' is a 'dramatically non-zero sum activity' (Schelling, 1984: 269*)*. It may be claimed that this is the decisive argument against exclusively or mainly relying on force to fight terrorism. This book argues that there are alternative anti-terrorism policies available based on a positive approach. Under the right conditions, such anti-terrorist policies evolve into *positive sum games*: as a result, both parties will be better off. Part III of this book puts forward three concrete proposals on how to undertake such a positive response to terrorism.

IS DETERRENCE EFFECTIVE?

In the literature on terrorism, there is wide agreement that reliance on force as anti-terrorism policy is ineffective. One of the leading scholars reaches a clear conclusion: 'There is also abundant evidence to show that repressive overreaction play into the hands of terrorists and, if prolonged, become totally counterproductive' (Wilkinson, 2000: 115). Another scholar similarly argues: 'Our most effective defense against terrorism will not come from surveillance, concrete barriers, metal detectors, or new laws' (Jenkins, 2000).

The use of force is, in most cases, unable to deter individuals from engaging in future terrorist activities. Moreover, successful coercion is often impossible to undertake. It only works if the actual and potential terrorists perceive that pursuing their violent actions is clearly worse than stopping violence. In some cases, the perceived disadvantages of ceasing terrorist activities are considered to be so great (in particular when giving up means that the death penalty looms large) that virtually no military threat will compel terrorists to stop their activities. Examples are the attempt of the Russians to force the Chechen terrorists and guerillas to capitulate, or Israel's attempt to stop suicide bombing and other Palestinian terrorism by using extreme forms of coercion.

The US air raids on the home and headquarters of President Gaddafi in 1986 were widely hailed as a successful example of anti-terrorist policy using strong military force. Empirical analyses of terrorist incidents before and after the raid on Libya do not indicate any significant reduction of terrorist activities in which that country was involved. After a brief pause, Libya seemed to become even more involved in international terrorism. No less than 15 incidents in 1987, and 8 in 1988 were connected to Libya, but the most dramatic subsequent event was the bombing of Pan Am flight 103 in 1988, crashing in Lockerbie and killing 278 persons. Of course, this evidence does not necessarily mean that the coercive policy failed. There may be various long-term and indirect effects, one being that European governments decided to take stronger action against possible Libyan terrorists and people supporting them.

However, an econometric analysis using vector-autoregressive intervention techniques (Enders and Sandler, 1993) was not able to find any noticeable long-term effect of Reagan's retaliatory policy on curbing terrorist attacks directed against American interests. What that policy did achieve was a *substitution* of terrorist activities directed towards less risky targets.

The conclusion that focusing on coercion is ineffective also applies more generally on an international scale. While the major powers (above all the United States) use their vast wealth in military weapons, the adversaries avoid exposing themselves to the coercers' strength. Rather, they tailor their actions to exploit the weaknesses of the major powers. One of the prime weapons of the weak is guerilla and terrorist warfare. The coercers are unable, or for political and economic reasons unwilling, to escalate the amount of force used.

As was pointed out in the first chapter, the terrorists may also not reach their goals. Despite the fact that neither of the two sides is successful, the conflict has turned into an extreme form of negative sum game, in which all participants are net losers. This is a tragic case of a prisoner's dilemma game, where each side pursues what they think to be their best strategy, but whose combined effects reach an unfortunate and negative outcome (see Chapter 3).

Despite many claims as to its effectiveness, deterrence may indeed be counterproductive. Based on a large number of cases, this position is supported by many scholars. To quote Wilkinson (2000: 115) again: 'There is a widespread misconception that using terror to defeat terror will ultimately work. On the contrary, the evidence is that this policy is counter-productive.' Another well-known terrorism researcher similarly states: '[A]ttempts by the ruling regime to deter further violence with a particularly harsh exemplary punishment backfired catastrophically' (Hoffman, 1998: 61). But why is deterrence policy so often used when it does not work or is even harmful to the coercer? The answer lies in the incentives faced by governments. When a terrorist attack takes place, the government is expected by the citizens to undertake swift, decisive action. The use of counterforce is best suited to that purpose. It demonstrates that the government is determined to act and provides a 'macho' image. In contrast, more beneficial approaches (such as the ones discussed in Part II of this book) tend to be less spectacular and often need considerable time to be achieved. To move beyond deterrence requires adequate political institutions, allowing the government to undertake anti-terrorist policies which are fruitful in the long term.

ECONOMIC SANCTIONS

As an alternative to, or in combination with, imposing cost on actual or potential terrorists and the countries affiliated to them, it has often been argued that economic sanctions should be used. Economic sanctions on countries supporting and harbouring terrorists consist of restrictions on a country's imports and exports, either by boycotting all trade or particular commodities.

Objectives and Use

Negative economic sanctions put pressure on the adversary to change its policy. Using economic sanctions only makes sense in the case of state sponsored terrorism. If the target country is unable to control, or at least influence, the behaviour of the terrorists located in their country, sanctions cannot possibly have any effect.

The economic pressure generated, and the damage done to the country as a whole, is intended to create widespread discontent. This, in turn, should induce the government to undertake the policies desired by the coercer. In particular, the boycotted countries should break all links to the terrorists in question and possibly hand them over to the coercer or to an international court.

Sanctions are used as a matter of course during wars. They are designed to cut off the flow of arms, the importation of natural resources and spare parts, and to decrease economic production, thereby also curbing arms production. Sanctions have often been used by the major powers, in particular by the United States and the United Nations, recent examples being in Afghanistan, Iraq, Libya and Somalia. The 1990s saw more than 50 applications of international economic sanctions.

Conditions for Success

It is useful to distinguish between three types of requirements in order for economic sanctions to have any effect.

Organisational conditions
Economic sanctions must be imposed by all major trading nations in order to prevent the boycotted country from compensating by importing from, and exporting to, countries not participating in the

embargo. In principle, the sanctions should be universal, because actors breaking the embargo can reap substantial profits. The incentive to free-ride in the case of collective sanctions must be overcome. But, as such profit opportunities can be reaped by 'footloose' private entrepreneurs acting at an international level, it is difficult, if not impossible, to suppress such undermining trade.

Economic sectors previously exporting goods to the now boycotted country will suffer losses. These burdens must be shared more generally because otherwise the sanctioning policy will not be politically accepted, and will soon be avoided. In addition, the list of sanctioned goods must be broad enough to limit possible substitution by the boycotted country.

Economic conditions
Sanctions only have a noticeable effect on an economy if production and consumption are inflexible. In general, however, this is not the case. Indeed, experience has shown that there are many possibilities for substituting goods in production and consumption, and also for switching to domestic production instead of importing. Not to exploit the advantages of international specialisation involves additional costs. But these costs tend to be rather small.

Political conditions
Even when sanctions have a strong effect on the economy, they only bring about the desired change in policy if the government's political position is threatened. This is unlikely to be the case, because the economic burdens are being imposed by a foreign power. The government can mobilise nationalistic feelings, and thereby produce a 'rally around the flag' effect in their favour. The potential or actual political opposition parties in a given country have little chance of proposing an alternative policy, as they can be charged with betraying their country. In that case, economic sanctions are counterproductive. The government's domestic position is strengthened, making it more unlikely that the policy of support for terrorism will be altered. Moreover, in many less developed countries, the authoritarian rulers own the firms, either directly or indirectly. By engaging in breaking the boycotts, they can reap huge profits, which may be used to solidify their political position.

Are Economic Sanctions Effective?

The discussion of the three types of conditions has shown that sanctions are unlikely to achieve their stated political goals. The most extensive study (Hufbauer, Schott and Elliott, 1990) analyses 103 cases of economic sanctions occurring between 1914 and 1990, and considers 34 per cent of them to have been successful in terms of their effect on the changes in the policies and capabilities of the target countries. But many other scholars have criticised the overall effectiveness of sanctions. In a more recent study, the authors seem to revise their views as they state: 'the history of economic sanctions reveals very few instances in which economic weapons achieved major foreign policy aims' (Hufbauer, Schott and Oegg, 2001: 2). Further studies demonstrate that even widely applied sanctions have had only moderate effects on the economy. A major reason is that the money used for the economic transactions is the ultimate fungible asset, opening up innumerable opportunities for undermining the boycotts. The black market can be used, investments can be redirected from sanctioned to unsanctioned sectors, and all sorts of substitutions can be undertaken. But an even weaker aspect of economic sanctions is that the burdens imposed on the population of the targeted country can rarely be used to affect a change of policy in the desired direction.

One of the most prominent recent uses of economic sanctions has been against Saddam Hussein's regime in Iraq, undertaken before the invasion of American and British forces in 2003. The sanctions were imposed by UN Security Resolution 687 to force Iraq to eliminate all its weapons of mass destruction and missiles. The sanctions may have actually strengthened, rather than weakened, Saddam's grip on power. He used the Iraqi food stockpiles, as well as the black market, to increase his support among the military forces and secret police. At the same time, the UN official who coordinated the oil-for-food programme claimed that half a million children died as a result of the sanctions. The economic sanctions against Iraq were not only counterproductive, but also debatable on moral grounds.

Are Targeted Sanctions the Solution?

The failure of broad sanctions to effect desired policy changes has led to attempts to target the boycotts more specifically in order to reach the goals.

Smart sanctions

Only those exports to the target country directly serving to bring about the desired policy change are to be prohibited. The country must be prevented from importing goods helping it to build up its military and police potential. Most importantly, the import of components and spare parts used to produce biological, chemical and nuclear weapons of mass destruction must be stopped, as there is a possibility of them being delivered to, or stolen by, terrorists. In contrast, goods serving the needs of the population as a whole, such as food and medical supplies, may be freely exported to the target country.

At first sight, smart sanctions seem to be a good idea. They are aimed at the undesired activities of the government, but do not punish the innocent population at the same time. Unfortunately, smart sanctions are unlikely to work in this way, and they are unable to drive a wedge between the government and the population in the target country. The reason is that partial economic sanctions open up many opportunities for substitution. Consider medical supplies. If these are shipped to the target country, they can always be seized by the government, sold on the international (black) market, and the foreign exchange received used to buy military weapons. Even if such resale could be prevented, smart sanctions would still not work, because the government of the target country can resort to internal substitution. In many cases the target country has imported some medical supplies before the smart sanctions. If this is the case, the government can now substitute them for the imports allowed under the smart sanctions. The foreign exchange saved can then be used to import goods useful for military and police purposes.

Financial boycotts

The targeted country's policy can be influenced by interfering in its financial dealings. It must be prevented from acquiring foreign exchange which can be used to acquire arms on the international (black) market. But experience demonstrates that barter can quite easily be substituted for foreign exchange. Goods are directly traded for other goods, sometimes in a whole series of exchanges. Preventing the use of foreign exchange imposes some costs on the targeted country, but they certainly do not seem to be large enough to bring about a change in policy.

It must be concluded that, while targeted sanctions look promising, they are unlikely to reach their stated objective. They are as ineffective as general economic sanctions. This conclusion certainly holds if they are undertaken as the only instrument of anti-terror policy. They may work better when applied in combination with other means.

IS DETERRENCE A GOOD ANTI-TERRORIST POLICY?

Most observers agree that deterrence is not effective in changing the target country's policy towards terrorism. But it does not follow that coercion should not be used to fight terrorism. It is mistaken to focus primarily on 'effectiveness', as is done in much of the literature on terrorism. There are four major reasons for this.

'Success' is Ill-defined

The concept of 'effectiveness' is wrong in suggesting that the criteria for success are given. It is assumed as a matter of course that 'success' means that potential terrorists and the targeted country change their policy in the direction desired by the coercing country. But this assumes countries as a whole to be the actors. Such an approach is mistaken, because persons can only act in the sense of evaluating benefits and costs, or success. What is considered a success from the point of view of one actor may well be a failure from the point of view of another actor. Even if deterrence proved to be 'counterproductive' for the coercing country, this does not necessarily mean that the government would refrain from applying a deterrence policy. The government often sees deterrence as the only way of signalling to its own people that it is determined to fight terrorism at 'all costs'. Not doing so may result in a loss of votes and so threaten the government's survival.

Costs are Neglected

When a policy is evaluated in terms of 'effectiveness', the cost side is totally neglected. A particular anti-terrorist policy, such as deterrence, may sometimes be effective in the short run, but its economic, political and moral costs may be prohibitive. In contrast, economic sanctions may, at least at the beginning, entail rather low costs for the coercing country, but that does not mean that they are therefore advisable.

Evaluation is Absolute

The discussion in the prevailing literature of whether deterrence policy is effective is couched in absolute terms. Deterrence is compared to no deterrence. The extreme cases of no deterrence or total deterrence in most cases are an irrelevant policy option. The politically relevant choice is, if anything, between more or less deterrence. This means that a marginal evaluation of the benefits and costs of a particular policy should be undertaken.

Alternatives are Missing

The existing literature suggests that deterrence has at best little and uncertain effect. But such evaluation has to be compared to the alternatives available, such as those proposed in the third part of this book. A worthwhile evaluation must make an effort to compare the use of force with more positive anti-terrorist policies.

The four objections to judging deterrence policy in terms of effectiveness leave open whether or not it should be recommended as an instrument for overcoming terrorism. In order to be able to deal with this issue, Part II (Chapters 3 and 4) develops an 'Economic approach to terrorism'. It constitutes a particular approach to analysing terrorism. By its very nature, this way of thinking considers how *individual* decision-makers are affected by the various anti-terrorist policies; it takes both benefits and costs of policies into account; and uses a *marginal* evaluation. Part III (Chapters 5, 6 and 7) presents *alternatives* to deterrence policy. Only on that basis can firm conclusions be drawn on the policies to overcome terrorism (Part IV).

SUGGESTED FURTHER READING

The variety of response modes to terrorism are discussed, for instance, in:

Schmid, Alex P. and Ronald D. Crelinsten (eds) (1993). *Western Responses to Terrorism*. London: Frank Cass.

The differentiation between coercion and brute force is due to:

Schelling, Thomas C. (1966). *Arms and Influence*. New Haven, CT: Yale University Press.

The case of the US raid on Libya is dealt with in:

Lesser, Ian O., Bruce Hoffman, John Arquilla, David F. Ronfeldt, Michele Zanini and Brian Michael Jensen (1999). *Countering the New Terrorism*. Santa Monica, CA: Rand Corporation, pp. 111–13.
Schmid, Alex P. and Ronald D. Crelinsten (eds) (1993). *Western Responses to Terrorism*. London: Frank Cass, pp. 315–17.

The econometric analysis of the long-run consequences of the attack on Libya is due to:

Enders, Walter and Todd Sandler (1993). 'The Effectiveness of Antiterrorism Policies: A Vector-Autoregression-Intervention Analysis'. *American Political Science Review* **87** (4): 829–44.

The use of military force as the only effective counter-strategy against terrorism is, for instance, advocated by:

Carr, Caleb (2002). *The Lessons of Terror. A History of Warfare against Civilians: Why It Has Always Failed and Why It Will Fail Again*. New York: Random House.
Harmon, Christopher C. (2000). *Terrorism Today*. London: Frank Cass.

The costs of deterrence in terms of human and political rights are, among others, discussed in:

Rathbone, Anne and Charles K. Rowley (2002). 'Terrorism'. *Public Choice* **111** (1–2): 9–18.
Wilkinson, Paul (2000). *Terrorism Versus Democracy: The Liberal State Response*. London: Frank Cass.
Cole, David and James X. Dempsey (2002). *Terrorism and the Constitution. Sacrificing Civil Liberties in the Name of National Security*. New York: The New Press.
Chang, Nancy (2002). *Silencing Political Dissent. How Post-September 11 Anti-terrorism Measures Threaten Our Civil Liberties*. New York: Seven Stories Press.
Falk, Richard (2003). *The Great Terror War*. New York and Northampton, MA: Olive Branch Press.

An attempt at empirically measuring the trade-offs implied has been undertaken after September 11, 2001, by:

Viscusi, W. Kip and Richard J. Zeckhauser (2003). 'Sacrificing Civil Liberties to Reduce Terrorism Risks'. *Journal of Risk and Uncertainty* **26**(2–3): 99–120.

The analysis of governments exploiting terrorist attacks for their own benefit is based on the Public Choice approach to politics. See for example:

Mueller, Dennis C. (ed.) (1997). *Perspectives on Public Choice*. Cambridge: Cambridge University Press.
Mueller, Dennis C. (2003b). *Public Choice III*, 3rd edn. Cambridge: Cambridge University Press.

The discussion of the partly counterproductive effect of Israeli raids on Palestinian terrorist organisations is taken from:

Byman, Daniel L. and Matthew C. Waxman (2002). *The Dynamics of Coercion. American Foreign Policy and the Limits of Military Power*. Cambridge: Cambridge University Press, p. 64.

Studying social interaction in terms of positive and negative sum games has long ago been applied to conflict theory by Boulding in:

Boulding, Kenneth E. (1962). *Conflict and Defense*. New York: Harper & Row.
Boulding, Kenneth E. (1973). *The Economy of Love and Fear*. Belmont, CA: Wadsworth.

The view that deterrence is an ineffective, and even counterproductive, counter-terrorist policy is, for instance, articulated in:

Wilkinson, Paul (2000). *Terrorism Versus Democracy: The Liberal State Response*. London: Frank Cass.
Hoffman, Bruce (1998). *Inside Terrorism*. New York: Columbia University Press.
Schmid, Alex P. and Ronald D. Crelinsten (eds) (1993). *Western Responses to Terrorism*. London: Frank Cass, pp. 315–17.

This applies, in particular, when the civilian population is affected. See:

Carr, Caleb (2002). *The Lessons of Terror. A History of Warfare against Civilians: Why It Has Always Failed and Why It Will Fail Again*. New York: Random House.

The generalisation of the use of force in the international system is dicussed in:

Byman, Daniel L. and Matthew C. Waxman (2002). *The Dynamics of Coercion. American Foreign Policy and the Limits of Military Power.* Cambridge: Cambridge University Press, p. 64.

The limits of applying negative sanctions between nations are highlighted in:

George, Alexander L. and William E. Simon (eds) (1994). *The Limits of Coercive Diplomacy.* Boulder, CO: Westview Press.
Cortright, David (1997). *The Price of Peace. Incentives and International Conflict Prevention.* Lanham, MD: Rowman & Littlefield.
Baldwin, David A. (1999). 'The Sanctions Debate and the Logic of Choice'. *International Security* **24** (3): 80–107.

The importance of mutually beneficial bargains for deterrence to be applicable was worked out in the 1960s by Schelling:

Schelling, Thomas C. (1966). *Arms and Influence.* New Haven: Yale University Press.

The stringent conditions for the success of economic sanctions are discussed in:

Frey, Bruno S. (1984). *International Political Economics.* Oxford: Blackwell.

Important economic analyses of economic sanctions are:

Elliott, Kimberly Ann and Gary Clyde Hufbauer (1999). 'Same Song, Same Refrain? Economic Sanctions in the 1990s'. *American Economic Review* **89** (2): 403–8.
Van Bergeijk, Peter A.G. (1994). *Economic Diplomacy, Trade, and Commercial Policy: Positive and Negative Sanctions in a New World Order.* Aldershot: Edward Elgar.
Kaempfer, William and Anton Lowenberg (1992). *International Economic Sanctions.* Boulder, CO: Westview Press.

A more general study is:

Hufbauer, Gary Clyde, Jeffrey J. Schott and Kimberly Ann Elliott (1990). *Economic Sanctions Reconsidered: History and Current Policy*, 2nd edn. Washington, DC: Institute for International Economics.

The case for the economic sanctions against Iraq is analysed in:

Byman, Daniel L. and Matthew C. Waxman (2002). *The Dynamics of Coercion. American Foreign Policy and the Limits of Military Power.* Cambridge: Cambridge University Press.

A particularly outspoken critic of economic sanctions is:

Pape, Robert A. (1997). 'Why Economic Sanctions Do Not Work'. *International Security* **22** (2): 90–136.
Pape, Robert A. (1998). 'Why Economic Sanctions Still Do Not Work'. *International Security* **23** (1): 66–77.

The possibilities and limitations of targeted sanctions are discussed in:

Hufbauer, Gary Clyde and Barbara Oegg (2000). 'Targeted Sanctions: A Policy Alternative?' *Law and Policy in International Business* **32** (1): 11–20.

Financial sanctions are the topic of:

Bierstecker, Thomas J. (2002). 'Targeting Terrorist Finances: The New Challenges of Financial Market Globalization'. In Ken Booth and Tim Dunne (eds). *Worlds in Collision: Terror and the Future of Global Order*. London: Palgrave: 74–84.

PART II

An Economic Approach to Terrorism

Economics has rarely dealt with terrorism, but Chapter 3 argues that this discipline opens up a useful avenue. It provides a further extension of the economic approach, which goes beyond the economy to cover other social issues. Terrorists are taken to be rational in the sense of systematically responding in their behaviour to changes in constraints, in particular those induced by anti-terrorist policies. Game theory is particularly useful for analysing the interaction between several governments fighting terrorism.

The individualistic economic approach, based on rational choice, differs substantially from other avenues, such as functionalist and psychological theories of terrorism.

Chapter 4 uses a very simple graph to illustrate the decision situation terrorists face as they compare the benefits to the costs incurred if they indulge in violent acts. The resulting equilibrium is defined by the equality of marginal benefits and marginal costs and corresponds to the rate of terrorist acts taking place.

The impact of anti-terrorist policies is reflected by shifts in the marginal benefit and cost curves, resulting in varying amounts of terrorist acts. Deterrence policy raises the material marginal costs to terrorists, and tends to reduce the number of terrorist acts. However, it is likely that the marginal benefit curve is also shifted upwards, so that it is uncertain whether the extent of terrorism falls or rises (counterproductive effect). Anti-terrorist policies relying on a positive approach are better suited to reducing terrorism. Providing alternatives to terrorists raises the marginal opportunity costs to terrorists. Decentralisation of the economy and polity, as well as reducing media attention to terrorists, lower the marginal benefits to terrorists, thus reducing the number and intensity of terrorist acts.

3. Terrorism Analysed

THE ECONOMIC APPROACH TO TERRORISM

What Is It?

The term 'economic' has two quite different meanings. On the one hand, it designates a *part of society*, the economy. On the other hand, it refers to a *discipline*, economics. This academic field is characterised by a particular way of looking at society. The term 'economic' is in this chapter to be understood in the second way, namely as the discipline of economics.

The economic way of thinking starts with individuals having goals (called preferences) and acting in a particular environment (being subject to restrictions). The major constraints individuals face are the time given (a day has 24 hours), the income received and assets one can dispose of, the limited mental capacities (for instance the bounded cognitive faculties to deal with complex issues) and the institutional conditions (such as the extent of the market sphere or democratic participation rights). Individuals behave in an uncertain world. Information is only gathered to the extent that it is perceived to be useful; the economic approach does not assume that individuals are fully informed.

Individuals are taken to be able to cope well with the decisions required to successfully pursue their own aims, taking into account the restrictions imposed from outside. They are assumed to maximise their own utility, subject to constraints. Individuals act consistently, and in this sense behave rationally.

This model of human behaviour has been applied to many different issues. It characterises human action not only in the economy, but also in politics, and in social interactions, such as in the family. In addition to narrowly conceived economics (the spheres of material production and consumption) 'rational choice analysis' has been applied to other areas, such as education, the natural environment, political decision-making, the family, and even to sport, religion and the arts. The approach has been introduced into other disciplines; in political science it is known as 'Public Choice' or '(New) Political Economy'; in sociology as 'Rational Choice'; and in law as 'the Economics of Law' or 'Law and Economics'. The theories of conflict and of peace and war have been strongly influenced by the economic approach. In the same spirit, there is also an 'Economic Theory of Terrorism'.

Rational Terrorists?

The basic concept applied to terrorists
It will probably come as a surprise to many readers to see terrorists being categorised as rational persons. This seems to be especially awkward in the case of suicide bombers, who are prepared to sacrifice their lives to further their cause. As they are dead when the results (possibly) occur, they cannot, so it seems, derive any satisfaction from their act.

The analysis of the motivations of terrorists nevertheless suggests that to assume rationality makes sense. Perpetrators undertaking suicide bombings are, in most cases, religious and nationalistic fanatics, who consider such attacks as part of a 'Holy War', which is divine will. Members of the Islamic terrorist group, *Hamas*, do not consider such attacks as suicide; rather they see themselves as martyrs (*shahid*) dying in the process of fulfilling a religious duty. The respective persons reap substantial rewards. They are guaranteed eternal life in paradise, will see the face of Allah, will (in the case of males) receive the loving care of 72 young virgins, and earn the privilege of enabling 70 relatives to enter paradise. Social rewards take the form of honour and praise and therefore a higher status being accorded to his or her family after his or her self-sacrifice. There are even material rewards, as the family receives financial compensation (allegedly 10,000 to 20,000 dollars). Suicide bombers thus receive considerable benefits from their act. Moreover, the potential suicide bombers are made to enter small terrorist cells under a charismatic leadership whose members become a peer group exerting social pressure. Before embarking on the sucide attack, the terrorists engage in a social contract, often in the form of a video testament. The institutional setting is thus of considerable importance in suicide terrorism. In view of these facts, it is therefore not surprising that the Palestinian (the *Hamas* and the Islamic *Jihad*), Tamil and Chechen terrorist groups have little or no problem in finding people ready to die for their beliefs.

But even without relying on such religious, social and material incentives, it is possible to explain the suicidal behaviour of terrorists. All individuals are to some extent prepared to give up some of their autonomy for solidarity with other persons (Wintrobe, 2002a,2002b). In the extreme, members of a terrorist group are increasingly giving up their identities for that of the group. They lose the capacity to make decisions deviating from those of the terrorist leaders, as their own values become completely identical. A member of such a terrorist group is rationally capable of committing suicide for the benefit of his or her group.

A more direct approach is to rely on the observation that these people have two kinds of motivations for their behaviour. On the one hand, they are extrinsically motivated by the religious, social and material rewards received. On the other hand, they are intrinsically motivated and take the necessary action simply because they want to, or because they have internalised social norms. Without doubt, terrorists are not solely induced by expectations of personal benefits, but have a substantial amount of intrinsic motivation.

The concept of rationality in economics does not depend on the particular content of individual utility functions. What matters is that individuals respond in systematic ways to changes in the constraints. Law-abiding citizens and terrorists may have very different goals, but they both react in the same way: when a particular activity becomes more costly to carry out, one increasingly undertakes less costly activities. This is the *generalised relative price effect* fundamental to economic reasoning. While the strength of the reaction may differ, the direction of the effect applies to all persons. This is the systematic element in human behaviour; it is not seen as mindless, crazy or solely subject to short-term emotions.

Following economics, rationality is completely independent of any moral judgment. To state that terrorists, and even suicide bombers, are rational in no way implies that their goals are 'rational'. The rational choice approach refrains from a normative judgement and seeks to understand *why* people – including terrorists – act as they act.

This approach, based on the behaviour of individuals, allows not only an analysis of the internal workings of a terrorist group, but also of the government fighting terrorism. Within terrorist groups, one often observes strong tensions and conflicts in need of explanation. It is useful to distinguish between persons in command, the active cadre, the rank and file, and the social environment, composed of various degrees of active and passive supporters. They certainly do not have identical goals as they are subject to different benefits and costs when acting.

Rationality by substitution

A more elaborate model of human behaviour, based on incentives, has been called RREEMM; it distinguishes the following aspects relevant for the study of terrorist behaviour:

- *Restricted*: terrorists are constrained by time and the material resources available to them, as well as their cognitive and physical abilities;
- *Resourceful*: terrorists are able and willing to consider alternative actions in response to changing opportunities;
- *Evaluating*: terrorists compare different alternatives with each other and choose those yielding the highest net benefits according to their utility function;
- *Expecting*: terrorists are not committed to short-run volitions, but are able to react in the long term;
- *Maximising*: terrorists systematically compare the marginal benefits and marginal costs of their actions (but, of course, they do not perform any explicit maximising calculus);
- *Man*, in the sense of a human being.

As close observations of the history of terrorism reveal, these aspects apply to both potential and actual terrorists. It has also been empirically shown that the generalised relative price effect following from these premises does indeed characterise terrorist behaviour. In particular, terrorists are able to *substitute* more costly targets in terms of the probability of being caught and the level of punishment with less costly targets. This means that their behaviour can be explained in a satisfactory way by the subjective expected utility model.

One of the first studies (Landes, 1978) applying this approach to terrorism empirically analysed the hijackings of aircraft in the United States in the period 1961–76. An increased likelihood of apprehension, as well as longer prison sentences, reduced the level of that particular kind of terrorism. The installation of metal detectors in US airports in 1973 is calculated to have reduced the number of hijackings by between 41 and 50 during period 1973–76. But this policy is likely to have induced other kinds of terrorist activities where the risk is lower.

This has indeed been found in a subsequent econometric study (Enders and Sandler, 2003), examining a broader set of anti-terrorist policies and terrorist activities. A similar substitution of means took place when the US embassies and missions the world over were heavily fortified. The terrorists adapted to this policy by increasingly assassinating diplomatic and military personnel *outside* protected compounds.

Substitution effects also take place on the side of potential victims. As discussed in Chapter 1, tourists choose their holiday destinations with due consideration of the perceived danger of a terrorist attack; the same substitution effect has also been shown to occur for foreign direct investment.

It is useful to distinguish four different substitution effects. Terrorists substitute with respect to

- *Targets*: they choose objects which are easier (less costly) to attack;
- *Modes of attack*: terrorists switch to those types of attack which are less costly in view of the anti-terrorist policies undertaken;
- *Countries*: terrorists engage in violent acts in those countries where the chances of success are higher;
- *Over time*: terrorists deplete the resources at their disposal and therefore have to wait until they can rebuild their capacity. This leads to cycles in terrorist activities.

The substitution effects document the fact that terrorists' behaviour can indeed be analysed in terms of rational decision processes.

Is there any irrational behaviour?

Some scholars of terrorism are convinced that terrorists are mentally deranged. Consider this quote: 'most murderers and terrorists are to one extent or other abnormal . . . it is important to establish the mental deviation or sheer aberration of many terrorists' (Parry, 1976: 26). The following six psychological types have been described to be most likely to threaten and try to use weapons of mass destruction: paranoids, paranoid schizophrenics, borderline mental defectives, schizophrenic types, passive-aggressive personality types and sociopath personalities. The last type is seen to be the most dangerous. However, even if these abnormal or mentally ill persons want to commit terrorist acts, they are less likely to actually try them, or to be successful when they do try. However, most psychologists who have done research on terrorism, have come to the conclusion that there is no identifiable terrorist mindset. It is not possible to find any convincing relationship between so-called abnormality and terrorist behaviour. Most sociopathic, schizophrenic and paranoid personalities never consider terrorist acts, and most terrorists have completely normal mindsets. One major expert on terrorism opens his book with this statement: 'I have been studying terrorists and terrorism for more than twenty years. Yet I am still always struck by how disturbingly "normal" most terrorists seem when one actually sits down and talks to them' (Hoffman, 1998: 7).

Terrorists are not generally wild-eyed fanatics or crazed killers, but rather persons reacting reasonably to the conditions they are exposed to. This makes terrorists *more* rather than less dangerous. They are able to react rationally to counter-terrorist policies, and sometimes are even able to pre-empt them. Indeed, one of the characteristics of terrorist groups is their capacity for innovation. They often act in a more enterprising way than do their counterparts in the bureaucratised police and military organisations.

The rational choice approach to terrorism does not assume that terrorists always act rationally in every situation. When, for instance, they are under heavy psychic and emotional strain, they may well react in an unpredictable and incoherent way. They are also subject to so-called 'anomalies of behaviour' – as we all are. Terrorist leaders succumb to the anomaly of using more resources and taking more risk than is good for them. They also tend to value sunk costs – the price they paid in the past – more than a strictly rational approach would suggest. Terrorist leaders also have high loss aversion, so that outside pressure may induce them to pursue failing strategies for longer than would be rational. Terrorists are also sensitive as to how coercive threats are framed. An identical policy may lead to different reactions, according to the way it is formulated and communicated.

It should be noted, however, that not only terrorist leaders are subject to such paradoxical behaviour. The same applies to politicians, public officials and military and police commanders making anti-terrorist decisions. An empirical study (Viscusi and Zeckhauser,

2003) has shown that normal citizens are not immune to behavioural anomalies when assessing the risk of terrorism. This is mainly due to the great uncertainty, or total ignorance, of the risk of possibly falling victim to a future terrorist attack. In the United States, over the period 1970–2000, the hijicking fatality rate per flight was just over 1 per 100 million flights, that is, it was extremely low. The hijackings of September 11, 2001 led to a sudden large upward reassessment of that risk, but people are at a loss as to exactly how much. In these circumstances, individuals were shown to be subject to the embedding effect: irrespective of whether individuals were asked to evaluate one risk or a larger category of many combined risks, they always made the same evaluation of how likely they consider a terrorist attack to be. People are also subject to hindsight bias: they believe that they knew the risk all along, although in reality the risk was completely unanticipated. They afterwards believe that they could have predicted a terrorist attack before it happened. Finally, people prove to react little or not at all to marginal changes in terrorism risks; they react only to a complete elimination of terrorism – a state of the world impossible to achieve. They attach too high a premium to complete certainty.

Behavioural anomalies on the part of all actors involved should, however, not be overrated. Most of the time, and in most circumstances, rational behaviour in the sense of systematic reactions to changes in incentives prevails. Behavioural anomalies should merely be considered as minor deviations. Moreover, persons who are aware that they are subject to anomalies in their own behaviour (and thereby undertake actions contrary to their own interests) can guard against them by following appropriate rules.

In terrorism, waves of imitative behaviour are sometimes observed, which seems to indicate the lack of rationality. Thus the first hijackings of aircraft were soon followed by other hijackings. But such imitation is not necessarily irrational. Once an innovation in terrorist tactics has been made, it is cheap to imitate, sparking off a whole wave of similar atrocities. If this is understood, decision-makers can react accordingly, but they must do so quickly.

Development of the Economics of Terrorism

The most influential precursor of the application of rational choice reasoning to the study of international relations and conflict is Tom Schelling. In his books *The Strategy of Conflict* (1960) and *Arms and*

Influence (1966), he demonstrated how the economic approach, and in particular applied game theory, can be used to gain insights into international conflicts going beyond those of international relations and political science. Kenneth Boulding is another economist making an early contribution in his book *Conflict and Defense: A General Theory* (1962), emphasising the concepts of equilibrium and strategic interaction in a simple game theoretic framework, as well as the dynamics characterising international interactions. Among the earliest contributions to the economics of terrorism are the game theoretic paper by Selten (1977) and the empirically oriented approach by Landes (1978). An important precursor and current contributor is also Jack Hirshleifer (1978), who was one of the first to apply evolutionary models originating in biology to international conflict and war.

The economic approach to analysing terrorism was for a long time a specialised subfield of international political economy scarcely known to traditional economics scholars. Yet, especially Todd Sandler, Walter Enders and their respective co-authors undertook interesting and relevant theoretical and empirical work. They published some of their findings in the leading journals in economics (such as the *American Economic Review*, the *Journal of Law and Economics* or *Kyklos*), in political science (such as the *American Political Science Review*) and in conflict theory (such as the *Journal of Conflict Resolution*). In addition to a general social science journal (*Terrorism and Political Violence*), there is also an economics journal (*Defence and Peace Economics*). Nevertheless, the work by economists on terrorism has not received the attention it deserves. In fact, few specialist authors on terrorism ever quote the contributions by economists (and, if at all, only the early works by Schelling).

Since the attacks on the World Trade Center in New York, research on terrorism has taken on ever greater significance. This also helped the economics of terrorism to become better known. Since that date, several scholars have started to engage in the subject and to present their results at general professional conferences, as well as in specialist meetings.

Game Theoretic Approach

The theory of strategic games obviously lends itself well to analysing the strategic interactions between countries and between countries and terrorists.

The basic issue of international terrorism may be couched in game theoretic terms. It is in the interests of every civilised nation to fight terrorism and to see that all other nations take a tough stance on terrorism. For example, aircraft hijackers' demands should never be granted, because such terrorist activity then becomes more attractive, thereby harming all other nations. But nations often renege on their promise to reject terrorists' demands when they are confronted with a terrorist incident. In such a case, it is often advantageous for the country targeted to yield to the demands and to let the terrorists escape unharmed. A world without terrorism is a public good from which all countries benefit. But each country has an incentive to free ride: the most favourable policy for each country is to let the others carry the costs of fighting terrorism and come to its own arrangements with the terrorists.

Consider the following simple *n*-person Prisoner's Dilemma game (Sandler, 1997). Five nations are confronted with a common terrorist threat from a nation sponsoring terrorists. The five nations promise in a treaty to punish the terrorist sponsor with retaliation should a terrorist incident occur. Each nation then has two strategies available; it can choose to honour or renege on the promise. Let's assume that each country keeping to the promise has retaliation costs of 8 and confers benefits in terms of deterrence of 5 on itself, as well as on the other nations in the treaty. These benefits from retaliation have the character of a public good. It automatically benefits all five nations in the pact (it is nonexclusive), and the fact that one nation benefits does not reduce the benefits to any other nation (it is nonrival).

The game matrix showing the decision situation for a representative nation is displayed in Figure 3.1.

In the case where nation *i* adheres to its promise when attacked by terrorists and the other *four* nations do so as well, nation *i* receives gross benefits of 25 (five times the benefits produced by the retaliating nations) minus the nation's cost of 8. The net benefits are 17, as shown in the matrix. In contrast, if nation *i* does not adhere to its promise to retaliate, it receives the free-rider payoff of 5 from each of the nations abiding by the treaty, adding up to 20.

If only country *i* and *three* other countries abide, nation *i* receives a net benefit of 12 (four times the benefit of 5 produced by the retaliating nations minus the cost of 8). If nation *i* reneges, it does not incur any costs of retaliation and gets a benefit of 15 (three times the benefits produced by the other retaliating countries of 5). The other

Number of treaty-abiding nations other than nation *i*

	0	1	2	3	4
Nation *i* abides by treaty	−3	2	7	12	17
Nation *i* does not abide by treaty	0	5	10	15	20

Source: Sandler (1997), Figure 4.9.

Figure 3.1   Fighting terrorism as a public good

payoffs can be calculated accordingly. For example, in the first column no other country honours its promise. Nation *i* is thus the only one abiding by the treaty, receiving gross benefits of 5, resulting from its own retaliation and having costs of 8, so that gross benefits are −3. But if the nation also reneges, as do all the other nations, it receives no benefits.

When comparing the benefits in the two rows, it can be seen that not abiding by the treaty *always* produces a higher net benefit to the representative country under consideration, regardless of how the other countries behave. As the situation is the same for each country, not to retaliate, that is not to abide by the treaty, is the *dominant* strategy nations pursuing their own self-interest must be expected to follow. As is the case in other Prisoner's Dilemma games, the cooperative outcome, in which each nation keeps its promise, is not attained, though for all the countries combined it provides the highest net benefits, namely 17 for each country. The self-interest of each nation is incompatible with the interests of the community of nations.

The Prisoner's Dilemma just discussed captures an important feature of international anti-terrorist policy. All civilised nations agree that terrorism should not be tolerated, and that one should not give in to the demands of terrorists. But practically every nation confronted with terrorism has, at times, reneged on its pledge never to negotiate with terrorists. This even applies to Israel, the strongest supporter of the principle of never negotiating with terrorists. But, in the case of kidnapped children at Maalot in May 1974, and in the case of TWA flight 847 in June 1985, exceptions were made. The same is true for the United States. Publicly, the Reagan administration called on all countries never to negotiate with terrorists in order not to encourage them and others to do the same again. But the same administration bartered arms for the release of hostages during 1985–86.

Repeated interactions are unlikely to solve the Prisoner's Dilemma situation outlined here. In principle, when the same situation is expected to occur a number of times in the indefinite future, the nations involved may agree to punish a country reneging on its promises. As no country knows what situation it will find itself in in the future (the veil of uncertainty reigns), such a resolution may be adopted by unanimous consent. However, in international relations, the punishment agreed on is unlikely to have much effect on a particular nation once it is attacked by terrorists. But politicians dependent on being re-elected still find it advantageous to renege and to start negotiations with the terrorists in order to save hostages, and more generally to keep current political costs low.

Another possibility to overcome Prisoner's Dilemmas is the effect of the costs of losing one's reputation in the international community when one reneges on treaties one earlier supported. However, the decision-makers are not countries as a whole, but rather politicians in a government, who care little about the future reputation falling on subsequent administrations, possibly made up of different, and even competing parties.

A policy never to negotiate with terrorists is not always advisable, as further game theoretic analyses have shown. The following assumptions must be met to make it effective:

- The government's decision never to negotiate must be completely credible to potential hostage takers;
- The outcomes (payoffs) of the various strategies must be known with certainty;
- The only benefit to terrorists must be the ransom derived from the exchange of the hostages. Other goals, such as media attention, must not play any role;
- The government's expenditures on deterrence must be large enough to deter most attacks.

These conditions are rather stringent and, in most cases, are unlikely to be fulfilled. It follows that the resolution to never negotiate with terrorists is not necessarily the best policy.

The basic situation faced by countries when dealing with terrorism has been couched in terms of a public good in which each country has an individual incentive to free ride. But there is another noncooperative option, *paid riding* (Lee, 1988). Each country can 'sell' the benefits from the retaliation of others by providing sanctuary to terrorists. They then commit no terrorist acts *within* the country, but continue to do so in foreign countries; thus the terrorist problem is effectively exported. Such a policy seems to have been undertaken by various countries, partly because they felt themselves unable to otherwise prevent terrorism within their borders.

Despite the fundamental problems faced by international agreements to fight terrorism, nations have formed many international conventions and resolutions to thwart terrorism, many of them in the context of the United Nations and addressed to hijacking aircraft and hostage taking. Empirical evidence suggests, however, that these conventions and resolutions were not able to produce any significant reduction in the number of skyjackings and hostage takings of protected persons. One of the major reasons is that, in order to gain the necessary support in the UN, the anti-terrorist treaties were forced to leave many loopholes. Treaties between neighbouring countries dealing with concrete cases and problems are actually more effective. A good example is the 1973 treaty between the United States and Cuba, where it was agreed to extradite or heavily punish terrorists who divert planes to either country. In this case, the common interests are clearly visible, and the negative consequences of reneging obvious.

Recently, the strategic interaction between governments and terrorists has been modelled by other typical games such as the Assurance Game. Also, evolutionary games take into account that the players involved learn from their experiences.

Without a doubt, the fundamental types of game – in particular the Prisoner's Dilemma game – provide important insights for a theory of terrorism. It is somewhat more doubtful whether more advanced gaming approaches (which nevertheless can integrate partial aspects of terrorism) provide as many additional insights.

ALTERNATIVE APPROACHES

Unit Actor Theories

Most theories on terrorism (outside economics and social psychology) look at aggregates as actors. Most importantly, nations are taken as actors in the international system. Thus 'Britain' or 'the United States' is seen as reacting in one way or another to terrorism, for instance, to impose coercive deterrence. Such a point of view is characteristic of international relations theory and is also common in much of sociology, political science and law. These disciplines have shaped the existing research on terrorism.

This approach implicitly assumes that the persons taking action pursue the interests of the unit they belong to, as no differentiation is made between the unit and its representatives. The politicians in government are assumed to pursue what is best for the country as a whole. The same applies to terrorist groups, where no differentiation is made between the individuals making up that group and the group as a whole.

The unit actor view makes sense in retrospect. When looking at past situations, one can reasonably ascribe a particular anti-terrorism policy to a particular nation, or a particular violent act to a particular terrorist group. As the disciplines just mentioned normally pay great attention to historical aspects, attributing actions to units is warranted. However, such an approach disregards differences in views, tensions and conflicts within the aggregate units. For instance, 'Britain' is by no means homogeneous with respect to deterrence policy. Indeed, many persons and subgroups strongly oppose using counter-terror to deal with terrorists. The views are, in most cases, not even uniform within the government. It is also known that terrorist groups are faced with considerable differences in opinion among their members and supporters. The leaders often pursue different goals from the rank and file, not to speak of the passive supporters. This means that when any future decisions are analysed, it may be important to first identify the benefits and costs of the alternative policy options as they affect individual actors, and then inquire how these divergent views can be aggregated in the social and political process.

Functionalist Theories

Another approach assumes that the fundamental purpose of any organisation, be it a terrorist group or the nation, is to maintain itself. Terrorist, national and governmental behaviour represents the outcome of the dynamics of the 'system' as a whole; no strategic action is implied. Viewing the international system and terrorism in this light may be revealing as a description of what has occurred in the past. It is less helpful when one considers reactions to the behaviour of other actors or to institutional changes. Moreover, it is not easy to explain why some terrorist groups, as well as some nations (for instance most recently the German Democratic Republic), disappear and how new actors (formerly unknown terrorist groups or new countries, such as recently Slovakia) emerge.

These alternative theories used to analyse terrorism deviate strongly from the economic or rational choice approach. All these approaches may well serve to highlight some aspects, and are less useful or incapable of dealing with other aspects. As the existing literature on terrorism has explored the unit actor and the functionalist approaches to a great extent, this book seeks to demonstrate the insights one may gain by focusing on the systematic reaction of persons to their individual benefits and costs when taking alternative courses of action.

Psychological Theories

This approach is concerned with the study of terrorists as individuals at the micro-level, in particular their personalities, beliefs, attitudes, motivation, and records as terrorists. The following major approaches can be distinguished.

- The frustration-aggression hypothesis, according to which terrorist aggression is a response to the frustration of various political, economic and personal needs and objectives. While this hypothesis is prominent in the literature and popular among a considerable number of lay people, many scholars have dismissed it as erroneous that aggression is always caused by frustration or, even more, that frustration always leads to aggression and terrorist action.
- The negative identity hypothesis argues that terrorists con-

sciously assume a negative identity. This involves a vindictive rejection of the role regarded as desirable and proper by an individual's family and community. People engage in terrorism as a result of feelings of helplessness and rage over the lack of alternatives.

- The narcissistic rage hypothesis assumes terrorists to be mentally ill and sees the reasons in early childhood development. If the primary narcissism is not neutralised by submitting it to testing in reality, the 'grandiose self' leads to individuals who are sociopathic and arrogant. Terrorism then occurs in the context of narcissistic injury.

Humiliating terrorists is counterproductive, because the basis for their activity lies in their sense of low self-esteem and humiliation.

Psychological theories can certainly contribute greatly to our understanding of the motivations of terrorists. But, as has been pointed out earlier in this chapter, it has not been possible to identify any clear mindset for terrorists. Thus it would be wrong to jump directly from psychological motivations to behaviour without taking social conditions and institutions into account.

SUGGESTED FURTHER READING

The economic approach to social issues was championed by Becker:

Becker, Gary S. (1976). *The Economic Approach to Human Behavior*. Chicago: Chicago University Press.

In that work, Becker assumed that changes in behaviour were solely driven by changes in constraints. More recently, he has been able to integrate changes in tastes into his framework. See:

Becker, Gary S. (1996). *Accounting for Tastes*. Cambridge, MA and London: Harvard University Press.
Becker, Gary S. and Kevin M. Murphy (2001). *Social Economics*. Cambridge, MA: Harvard University Press.

The economic way of thinking is also the subject of:

Kirchgässner, Gebhard (2000). *Homo Oeconomicus: Das ökonomische Modell individuellen Verhaltens und seine Anwendung in den Wirtschafts- und Sozialwissenschaften*, 2nd edn. Tübingen: Mohr (Siebeck).

Frey, Bruno S. (1999). *Economics as a Science of Human Behaviour*, 2nd revised and extended edn. Boston and Dordrecht: Kluwer.
Frey, Bruno S. (2001). *Inspiring Economics: Human Motivation in Political Economy*. Cheltenham, UK and Northampton, USA: Edward Elgar.

The behaviour of suicide terrorists is discussed in:

Hudson, Rex A. (1999). *The Sociology and Psychology of Terrorism. Who Becomes a Terrorist and Why?* Washington, DC: Federal Research Division, Library of Congress [Internet: http://www.fas.org/irp/frd.html].
Atran, Scott (2003). 'Genesis of Suicide Terrorism'. *Science* **299**: 1534–9.

Two economists provide interesting models of how a radicalisation can come about, resulting in suicide terrorism:

Wintrobe, Ronald (2002a). 'Can Suicide Bombers be Rational?' Paper prepared for the workshop on The Economic Consequences of Global Terrorism, organised by DIW Berlin, June 14–15, 2002.
Wintrobe, Ronald (2002b). 'Leadership and Passion in Extremist Politics'. In Albert Breton, Gianluigi Galeotti, Pierre Salmon and Ronald Wintrobe (eds). *Political Extremism and Rationality*. New York: Cambridge University Press, pp. 23–43.
Ferrero, Mario (2002). 'Radicalization as a Reaction to Failure: An Economic Model of Islamic Extremism'. Department of Public Policy and Public Choice Working Paper No. 33, University of Eastern Piedmont, Italy.
Ferrero, Mario (2003). 'Martyrdom Contracts'. Mimeo, Department of Public Policy and Public Choice, University of Eastern Piedmont, Italy.

An approach basically differing from rational choice is provided, for example, by:

Tololyan, Khachig (2001). 'Cultural Narrative and the Motivation of a Terrorist'. In David C. Rapoport (ed.). *Inside Terrorist Organizations*. London: Frank Cass, pp. 217–33.

But there are also many non-economists who stress that terrorists are far from mindless or crazy. For an extensive study, see:

Harmon, Christopher C. (2000). *Terrorism Today*. London: Frank Cass.

Behavioural anomalies and their consequences are discussed in:

Dawes, Robyn M. (1988). *Rational Choice in an Uncertain World*. San Diego, CA and New York: Harcourt, Brace, Jovanovich.

Applications to international relations are given by:

Levy, Jack S. (1996). 'Loss Aversion, Framing, and Bargaining: The Implications of Prospect Theory for International Conflict'. *International Political Science Review* **17** (2): 179–95.
Levy, Jack S. (1997), 'Prospect theory, rational choice, and international relations', *International Studies Quarterly*, **41**: 87–112.

Behavioural anomalies with respect to risks of terrorism are empirically analysed in:

Viscusi, W. Kip and Richard J. Zeckhauser (2003). 'Sacrificing Civil Liberties to Reduce Terrorism Risks'. *Journal of Risk and Uncertainty* **26** (2–3): 99–120.

A survey of the economic approach to terrorism, including game theoretic aspects, is provided in:

Sandler, Todd and Walter Enders (2002). 'An Economic Perspective on Transnational Terrorism'. *European Journal of Political Economy*, forthcoming.

See also the collection of articles in the special issue of the *European Journal of Political Economy*, 20 (2004).

The early economic analysis of hijacking is due to:

Landes, William A. (1978). 'An Economic Study of US Aircraft Hijackings, 1961–1976'. *Journal of Law and Economics* **21** (1): 1–31.

The subsequent econometric studies are due to Enders and Sandler. A survey of their approach and major results is provided in:

Enders, Walter and Todd Sandler (2003). 'What Do We Know about the Substitution Effect in Transnational Terrorism?' In Andrew Silke and Gaetano Ilardi (eds). *Terrorism Research: Trends, Achievements and Failures*. London: Frank Cass.

The view of terrorists as mentally ill people is proposed in:

Berkowitz, B.J. et al. (1972). *Superviolence: The Threat of Mass Destruction Weapons*. Santa Barbara, CA: ADCON Corporation.

Many scholars in disciplines other than economics also hold the opposing view that terrorists are 'normal' people. See, for example:

Hoffman, Bruce (1998). *Inside Terrorism*. New York: Columbia University Press.

Major early contributions to the economics of terrorism are:

Schelling, Thomas C. (1960). *The Strategy of Conflict*. Oxford: Oxford University Press.
Schelling, Thomas C. (1966). *Arms and Influence*. New Haven, CT: Yale University Press.
Boulding, Kenneth E. (1962). *Conflict and Defense*. New York: Harper & Row.
Tullock, Gordon (1974). *The Social Dilemma. The Economics of War and Revolution*. Blacksburg, VA: University Publications.
Hirshleifer, Jack (1978). 'Natural Economy versus Political Economy'. *Journal of Social and Biological Structures* **1** (4): 319–37.

Jack Hirshleifer has also recently published:

Hirshleifer, Jack (2001). *The Dark Side of the Force: Economic Foundations of Conflict Theory*. Cambridge: Cambridge University Press.

An important contribution is also:

Bernholz, Peter (1985). *The International Game of Power*. Berlin: Mouton.

The game theoretic discussion of the difficulties in fighting terrorism is based on:

Sandler, Todd (1997). *Global Challenges*. Cambridge: Cambridge University Press.

The substitution between target countries undertaken by terrorists is analysed in:

Sandler, Todd and Harvey E. Lapan (1988). 'The Calculus of Dissent: An Analysis of Terrorists' Choice of Targets'. *Synthese* **76**: 245–61.

The possibility of 'paid riding' has been analysed by Lee in:

Lee, Dwight R. (1988). 'Free Riding and Paid Riding in the Fight Against Terrorism'. *American Economic Review* **78**: 22–6.

The conditions for successful negotiations are to be found in:

Lapan, Harvey E. and Todd Sandler (1988). 'To Bargain or Not to Bargain: That Is the Question'. *American Economic Review* **78** (2): 16–21.

Corresponding empirical analyses are provided in:

Enders, Walter, Todd Sandler and Jon Cauley (1990a). 'Assessing the Impact of Terrorist-thwarting Policies: An Intervention Time Series Approach'. *Defence Economics* **2** (1): 1–18.

Enders, Walter, Todd Sandler and Jon Cauley (1990b). 'UN Conventions, Technology and Retaliation in the Fight Against Terrorism: An Econometric Evaluation'. *Terrorism and Political Violence* **2** (1): 83–105.

Evolutionary game theory is applied to terrorism in:

Arce M., Daniel G. and Todd Sandler (2003). 'An Evolutionary Game Approach to Fundamentalism and Conflict'. *Journal of Institutional and Theoretical Economics*, **159** (1): 132–54.

A discussion of various approaches to the study of terrorism is provided in:

Crenshaw, Martha (2001). 'Terrorism'. In Neil J. Smelser and Paul B. Baltes (eds). *International Encyclopedia of the Social and Behavioral Sciences*, Vol. 23. Amsterdam: Pergamon, pp. 15604–6.

A thorough treatment of the sociological and psychological views on terrorism can be found in:

Hudson, Rex A. (1999). *The Sociology and Psychology of Terrorism. Who Becomes a Terrorist and Why?* Washington, DC: Federal Research Division, Library of Congress [Internet: http://www.fas.org/irp/frd.html].

4. Putting Policies into Perspective

TERRORISTS' INCENTIVES

The rational choice approach used in economics can be illustrated by simple graphs. They help us to better understand the effects of changes in anti-terrorist policy. The graphs represent the benefits and the costs of undertaking terrorist acts from the point of view of (potential) terrorists. This allows us to analyse the extent of terrorist acts expected to occur on the basis of analytical reasoning.

We first look at the benefits prospective terrorists hope to gain from their acts of terrorism. The following section focuses on the marginal costs of undertaking terrorist acts and the third section merges the two sides and identifies the extent of terrorist acts expected to take place in equilibrium.

What Do Terrorists Gain?

Figure 4.1 depicts the *total benefits* and *marginal benefits* of terrorism to the prospective terrorists as a function of the extent and intensity of terrorism T.

The upper part of Figure 4.1 shows that the benefits received by terrorists are the greater the more terrorist acts are undertaken. But these benefits do not increase in a linear way; the additional benefits of additional terrorist acts are getting smaller and smaller. The reason is that terrorists first undertake those terrorist acts producing the greatest benefits. And afterwards have to choose targets promising smaller benefits to them.

The marginal benefit curve, MB, in the lower part of the figure reflects the benefits to terrorists of undertaking *additional* terrorist acts. Corresponding to the total benefit curve, the marginal benefit curve slopes downwards, both in the number and intensity of terrorist acts. But the marginal benefit curve need not necessarily slope downwards; one could imagine situations in which the society targeted becomes more and more affected by terrorism, so that stepping

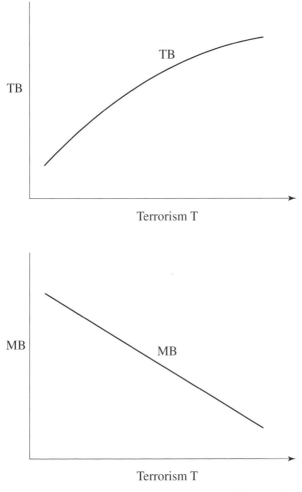

Figure 4.1 The total benefits (top) *and marginal benefits* (below) *to terrorists of committing terrorist acts*

up terrorism increases its marginal benefit. But this is unlikely to happen, because the persons and societies targeted learn to react to terrorist acts in such a way that the marginal effects tend to diminish. The persons potentially affected learn to avoid becoming targets, and make efforts to reduce the consequences of terrorist attacks. The position and slope of the marginal benefit curve for terrorism is thus not given; it also depends on the behaviour of the persons targeted.

To give these curves life and make them empirically relevant, the benefits of terrorism to terrorists need to be identified. Terrorism is often seen as a specific – namely a violent – form of political partici- pation. The ultimate aims of terrorism are, among others, the redis- tribution of power and property rights and the extortion of rents. To achieve this, terrorists seek to attain three main tactical goals:

1. Terrorists seek the *attention of the media* in order to make their cause more widely known. Terrorists seek to magnify their acts through the media.
2. Terrorists seek to *destabilise the polity*. When the government loses power and, more importantly, when the political system's legitimacy is eroded, the terrorists' chances of achieving their goals improve.
3. Terrorists seek to *damage the economy*. They want to impose material costs on the population in order to make them yield to their demands. The size of these effects for terrorist acts that have taken place in the past was discussed in Chapter 1. The more an economy is affected by terrorist acts, the higher is the terrorists' marginal benefit curve.

The three goals are intertwined. The extent of attention attributed to terrorist acts by the media affects both the polity and the economy. In all societies, the politicians in power react to the media (and therefore want to control them). The effect of the media on the economy works through consumers' and investors' expectations about the future state of business. The importance of terrorist acts is strongly shaped by how they are reported in the media. The more prominence they receive, the more strongly they depress expectations about the future state of the economy.

Economic conditions systematically affect the government, as has been empirically shown in the literature on popularity and election functions. A rise in unemployment and inflation, and a fall in the rate of growth in income, lower the survival prospects of the government. Bad economic conditions, a deep recession or depression, may even destroy the very constitutional foundations, and may encourage authoritarian or dictatorial governments to take over.

In order to achieve their goals, the terrorists undertake various types of action. One possibility is targeted attacks, for example assassination of a powerful political leader. Another possibility is attacks against targets with a high symbolic value. These may be well known monuments (such as the World Trade Center or St. Peter's in the Vatican) or global firms (such as McDonald's or Coca-Cola). A third possibility is to instil fear and panic among the people by attacking civilians (seemingly) at random.

The curves in Figure 4.1 represent the total and marginal benefits for a 'representative' terrorist. To answer more specific questions, it may be useful to construct corresponding (marginal) benefit curves for subsets of terrorists; say for the leaders, for the cadre, and for the supporters. Their benefits from undertaking additional terrorist acts may differ substantially from each other.

What Are the Costs to Terrorists?

The upper part of Figure 4.2 illustrates the *total* costs which the terrorists have to bear when they increasingly engage in terrorism. The costs increase, but in a more linear fashion.

The lower part of Figure 4.2 depicts the corresponding *marginal* costs. The *marginal cost* curve, MC, reflects the costs of engaging in *additional* terrorist acts. It slopes upwards because it is increasingly costly to undertake terrorist acts. To begin with, the easiest and most conveniently available targets are chosen. Thereafter, it becomes increasingly difficult to find worthwhile targets. The costs involved for the terrorists consist in human and material resources, gathering information, as well as the time needed to prepare for the attacks. Finally, costs also reflect the danger involved in actually undertaking the act. A terrorist may be hurt or lose his or her life while preparing or undertaking an attack, be captured, interrogated, possibly tortured, imprisoned or even put to death.

The marginal cost curve depends on the behaviour of terrorists. Two extreme assumptions may be made:

1. The persons engaging in terrorism are solely *extrinsically* motivated. They undertake their attacks because of the rewards they receive. In most cases, rewards are immaterial and take the form of gaining recognition and admiration from the persons supporting their cause. Many terrorists also enjoy the fame achieved in the international and local press. In some cases, terrorists receive

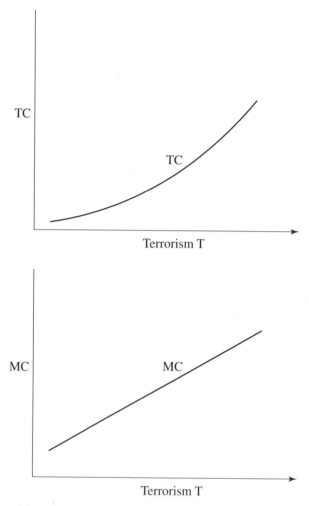

Figure 4.2 The total costs (top) *and marginal costs* (below) *to terrorists of undertaking terrorist acts*

monetary compensation for their acts, or their families are guaranteed financial support. Other rewards may be attractive political positions in the future and corresponding material and immaterial benefits in the case where terrorists are able to win over the existing government.

2. The prospective terrorists are solely *intrinsically* motivated. They are convinced they are doing the right thing, irrespective of any reward from outside. In many cases, this position is due to a social norm internalised by the individuals. If the 'representative' terrorist is motivated solely from within, the marginal cost curve would be steeper than it otherwise would be. This means that such persons react less to either costs or rewards for their actions.

Most (prospective and actual) terrorists are strongly influenced by their social environment, and react to externally offered incentives. Both extrinsic and intrinsic motives play a role. The marginal cost curve is thus positively sloped. It shifts upwards with an exogenous increase in the cost of undertaking terrorist acts.

The Theoretically Expected Extent of Terrorism

On the basis of the benefit and cost considerations shaping the curves, rational choice theory allows us to derive the expected intensity of terrorism. The terrorists aim at obtaining as many benefits as possible, but they take the cost to themselves into account. They seek to attain the largest net benefits. The difference between the benefit and cost curves are the highest where the marginal benefit and the marginal cost curve intersect. This is shown as point T_0^* in Figure 4.3.

This is an *equilibrium*, reflecting the most favourable extent of terrorism from the point of view of the terrorists. If they were to commit fewer violent acts than indicated by the equilibrium, they could improve their position, because additional terrorist acts bring them higher additional benefits than costs. Conversely, when they undertake more terrorist acts than indicated by the equilibrium, they incur higher additional costs than benefits. As terrorists are assumed to be rational in the sense discussed in the previous chapter, the equilibrium extent of terrorism corresponds to the actual amount of terrorism observed in reality.

Figure 4.3 and the resulting equilibrium are useful, because they allow us to see in a straightforward way how changes in conditions – reflected by *shifts* in the curves – affect the extent of terrorism (*comparative statics*). In the next section we look at the effects on terrorists of undertaking a coercive deterrence policy.

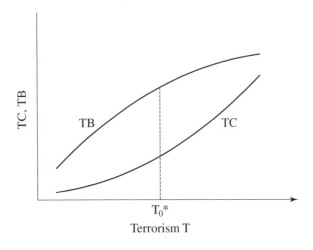

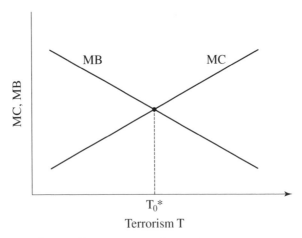

Figure 4.3   The equilibrium extent of terrorism

THE EFFECTS OF DETERRENCE POLICY

Deterrence policy seeks to raise the future costs of terrorist acts by making them more difficult to undertake and by punishing the actors more severely. An increase in the cost of terrorist activities can also be achieved indirectly by eliminating terrorists' resource base when they are at least to some extent state sponsored. The terrorists are

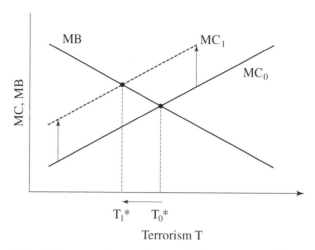

Figure 4.4   Deterrence changes the equilibrium amount of terrorism

robbed of their hiding places as 'safe havens'. Another possibility is to raise the cost to terrorists of financing themselves.

Figure 4.4 shows that a coercive deterrence policy shifts the marginal cost curve upwards. As a result, there will be a smaller equilibrium amount of terrorism.

In the (unlikely) event that terrorists are *solely* intrinsically motivated, they would not respond to negative incentives such as higher risk and more severe punishment. A deterrence policy would have less effect, because the marginal cost curve is then steeper than it would otherwise be. A deterrence policy is also ineffective if it is offset by rewards. This would be the case if prospective terrorists interpret a larger punishment as a signal that their cause is particularly worthy and will be rewarded accordingly in the afterlife.

But deterrence policy does not solely depend on the incentives of the potential terrorists. It also seeks to prevent terrorist acts by making them more difficult to undertake. A case in point is tightening up security measures to prevent the hijacking of aircraft and shipping.

The discussion suggests that, in many cases, a coercive deterrence policy is able to shift the perceived cost of terrorism upwards. It thereby reduces the intensity and number of terrorist acts. This is the reason why deterrence is at the forefront of anti-terrorist policy. Indeed, it is often taken to be the *only* possibility, both in the literature and in practical policy.

However, it must immediately be added that, in actual fact, it is not so easy to raise the costs of terrorism, because the terrorists have many means of substituting their activities and therefore avoiding much of the rise in costs intended by deterrence policy. Consider the effort to interrupt the source of the finances going to the terrorists. Such a policy was undertaken as a central part of the coercive response by the United States to *al Qaeda*'s attack on New York and Washington. The American administration froze a great number of assets and interrupted many monetary transfers. But *al Qaeda* has three main sources of finance: legitimate business, charitable donations and illegal activity. As it is as yet unknown what legitimate business activities are linked to *al Qaeda*, they are likely to fall outside the regulatory mechanisms to constrain terrorist asset transfers. The same holds for a centuries-old method of asset transfer, used particularly in South Asia, called *Hawala*. A large part of the monetary transfers from immigrant workers to their relatives at home occur through *Hawala* brokers. This method has the advantage of being reliable and cheap. Even if this very informal way of financial transfer could be controlled by a foreign power, it is highly likely that the transfer of assets for terrorist operations would find alternative ways.

Charitable organisations are even more difficult to control. It is almost impossible to distinguish the authentic from the terror affiliated. Financing from illegal activities is, by definition, almost impossible to monitor and to interrupt. There is a close analogy to the failing effort to successfully intervene in the flow of drug money. Indeed, some of the terrorist groups are intimately linked to the drug trade, the Colombian FARC being a pertinent example. But it is not too far-fetched to assume that *al Qaeda* is involved in the Afghanistan drug business that has blossomed after the defeat of the Taliban government. Well-organised terrorist groups, such as *al Qaeda*, use a nebulous, highly flexible and decentralised system. The terrorist cells located in target countries would appear to be financially self-sustaining.

An intervention in the financial system on the part of deterring countries also has indirect costs. If the system of *Hawala* is interrupted, or strongly interfered with, increased tensions with the (Arab) countries on the recipient side are unavoidable. Such action leads to negative effects on the economy of the recipient countries, possibly inducing them to take a more favourable stance towards the terrorists. The welfare level of the people decreases further if the Islamic charities providing humanitarian relief can no longer operate, or can operate only at a lower level. While it seems reasonable to try to interrupt the source of terrorists' finances, the corresponding attempts may easily lead to counterproductive effects.

Policies of fighting terrorism by the use of deterrence may backfire for yet another reason. A deterrence policy tends to *increase* political and economic centralisation. In order to curb terrorism by deterrence, the central government tends to reduce the democratic rights of citizens and to take power away from lower levels of government. The establishment of the US Department of Homeland Security constitutes just such a move towards bureaucratic centralisation. Increased expenditures for a coercive deterrence policy, moreover, benefit the military–industrial complex (to use President Eisenhower's term), which is far more centralised and monopolistic than other parts of the economy. More decision-making and implementation power is then vested in one location, making it vulnerable to terrorist attacks. Such a deterrence policy not only shifts the terrorists' cost curve upwards but, at the same time, also shifts their *benefit curve* upwards. The two effects are countervailing, and it remains open whether the equilibrium amount of terrorist activity actually falls, as is generally expected. It is quite possible that the increasing centralisation of the economy and polity raises a country's attraction to terrorists to such an extent that the equilibrium amount of terrorism *increases*. This situation is shown in Figure 4.5.

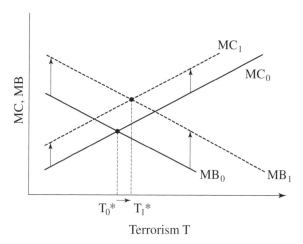

Figure 4.5   Coercive deterrence policy may increase terrorist activity

The lowering effect of deterrence is likely to dominate in the short term, but it may well be reversed over the long term. This should be taken into account by those prescribing a wise anti-terrorist policy.

THE EFFECTS OF ALTERNATIVE ANTI-TERRORIST POLICIES

There are alternatives to coercive deterrence policy that serve to effectively reduce the extent of terrorism. As they are based on a different approach, they do not have the disadvantages of deterrence policy we have outlined (but, of course, they may have other disadvantages).

Decentralising Political and Economic Activities

A country can be immunised against terrorist attacks by decentralising activity, with respect to both the polity and the economy. The basic idea is that a polity and society with many different centres is difficult to destabilise. Any particular centre is less essential for the polity and economy and therefore also of less symbolic value. If one of the centres is hit by a terrorist attack, other centres can take over the tasks. The attraction of violent actions on the part of terrorists is diminished, as they prove to have less effect on the political stability and aggregate economic activity.

Decentralising results in a downward shift of the marginal benefit function. Committing additional terrorist acts produces lower marginal utility to terrorists, because these acts achieve less. Figure 4.6 demonstrates that a downward shift in the marginal benefit curve to terrorists results in a *lower* equilibrium level of terrorist activities.

This policy option will be more fully discussed in Chapter 5.

Raising Opportunity Costs of Terrorists

An effective way to fight terrorism is to raise the *opportunity costs* to terrorists. It produces an upwards shift in terrorists' marginal cost curve of undertaking violent actions, and the expected extent of terrorist activity decreases. But this anti-terrorist policy differs fundamentally from traditional deterrence policy seeking to raise the

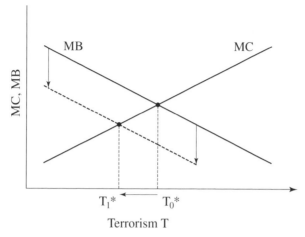

Figure 4.6 Decentralising reduces terrorism

material cost to potential terrorists. Indeed, the two approaches imply quite different policies.

The opportunity costs faced by potential terrorists consist in the utility they could gain by not engaging in terrorism. These are the activities they can undertake outside terrorism. Higher opportunity costs reduce the willingness of a (potential) terrorist to commit terrorist activities. An increase in the opportunity costs therefore reduces the amount of terrorism.

Such a strategy has several advantages over other anti-terrorist policies:

- Due to a wider scope of opportunities outside terrorist activities, a person's dependence on the terrorist group is reduced. Exit is facilitated.
- A conflict between the terrorist and other activities is created, which produces tensions within the terrorist organisation. Nobody knows who will succumb to the outside attractions and defect from the group. This diminishes the effectiveness of the terrorist group. In contrast, a deterrence policy strengthens solidarity among the group members.
- The interaction between the terrorists and all other people and groups is turned into a positive sum interaction. The chances of finding a peaceful solution are improved.

This policy will be more fully explored in Part Three of the book.

Reducing Media Attention

One of the central goals of terrorists is to gain the attention of the media in order to make their cause widely known. If it is possible to reduce such attention, terrorist acts become less attractive. As in the case of decentralisation (shown in Figure 4.6), the marginal benefit curve shifts *downwards*. The equilibrium extent of terrorism *falls*.

Chapter 7 presents a proposal for how media attention can be drawn away from the perpetrators of a terrorist act without resorting to control of the media.

SUGGESTED FURTHER READING

The difference between extrinsic and intrinsic motivation stems from social psychology. See, for instance:

Deci, Edward L. and Richard M. Ryan (1985). *Intrinsic Motivation and Self-determination in Human Behavior*. New York: Plenum Press.

The concept has also been integrated in economics. See:

Frey, Bruno S. (1997). *Not Just for The Money. An Economic Theory of Personal Motivation*. Cheltenham, UK and Brookfield, USA: Edward Elgar.

The financing of terrorist activities and the problems involved when trying to interfere are discussed in:

Huang, Reyko (2001). 'Mounting Costs of the Financial War Against Terrorism'. Mimeo, CDI Terrorism Project [Internet: http://www.cdi.org/terrorism/financial2-pr.cfm].
Lesser, Ian O., Bruce Hoffman, John Arquilla, David F. Ronfeldt, Michele Zanini and Brian Michael Jensen (1999). *Countering the New Terrorism*. Santa Monica, CA: Rand Corporation.

An estimate of the size of the underlying financial flows to terrorists has been ventured by:

Schneider, Friedrich (2004). 'Money for Terror: The Hidden Financial Flows of Islamic Terrorist Organizations'. *Defence and Peace Economics*: forthcoming.

See also:

Pieth, Mark (ed.) (2003). *Financing Terrorism*. Boston, Dordrecht and London: Kluwer.

PART III

Three Positive Policies for Dealing with Terrorism

A coercive response based on brute force is not the only anti-terrorism policy. This is important to realise, because deterrence policy is widely practised and is often thought to be the only possible and reasonable response. But exclusive reliance on deterrence policy is inadvisable as it:

- fails to be effective;
- involves very high costs in various ways to all parties involved; and
- may even be counterproductive, tending to increase terrorism.

The alternative anti-terrorism policies proposed here do not use an approach based on force. These policies are 'positive'; they do not seek to harm potential and actual terrorists, but nevertheless reduce terrorist activities.

The proposals are discussed according to how fundamental they are. The most basic anti-terrorism policy proposed in Chapter 5 emphasises the advantage of *polycentric* economic, political and social structures. A decentralised society is less vulnerable to terrorist attacks. This policy relies on society's fundamental institutions and involves constitutional arrangements.

Anti-terrorism policy can lure actual and prospective terrorists away from their deadly actions by providing *positive incentives* not to engage in those activities. The most important of such incentives proposed in Chapter 6 is the use of various methods to reintegrate potential perpetrators back into a civilised way of life.

Once a terrorist event has occurred, Chapter 7 discusses a proposal to *reduce the media attention* so avidly sought by the terrorists. This anti-terrorism policy is designed to strongly reduce the benefits to terrorists of engaging in violent actions.

5. Polycentricity Reduces Vulnerability

MAKING PROSPECTIVE TARGETS SAFER

A system composed of many different centres is more stable due to its variety, which enables parts to substitute for each other. When one part of the system is negatively affected, one or several other parts can take over. Polycentricity is effective in reducing risk and uncertainty. It corresponds to the old saying that it is wise 'not to put all your eggs in one basket'.

This basic insight from the field of socio-biology also applies to terrorism. A target's vulnerability is lower in a society composed of many centres than it is in a centralised society. The more centres of power there are in a country, the less terrorists are able to harm it. In a decentralised system, terrorists do not know where to strike, because they are aware that each part can substitute for the other, so that a strike is not likely to achieve much. Polycentricity thus reduces both the probability of terrorists launching an attack and the damage caused in case of an attack. For these two reasons, terrorists have a lower incentive to attack decentralised rather than centralised societies. In terms of the figures presented in the previous chapter, the marginal benefit curve from the point of view of the terrorists shifts downwards, resulting in a lower equilibrium extent of terrorist activity (see Figure 4.6).

In contrast, in a centralised system, most decision-making power with respect to the economy, polity and society takes place in one location. This central power is an ideal target for terrorists, and therefore is in greater danger of being attacked. This creates huge costs. If the centre is attacked and hit, the whole decision-making structure also collapses and promotes chaos. In addition, there are high costs in fending off possible attacks. They not only bind human and material resources, but also promote a bunker mentality in the minds of the central power. The ruler is driven into isolation, becomes subject to 'group think', and loses contact with the people. As a result, a gap between the central power and the people emerges, with bad effects on both. In particular, the ruler disregards the people's wishes, as he is afraid of leaving the bunker's (presumed) security.

The vulnerability of the two systems to terrorism varies and may be illustrated by two examples.

The attack on the World Trade Center in New York on September 11, 2001 represents a triumph for the market, although it is rarely seen in these terms. Though this was the gravest terrorist attack in mankind's history so far, the economic system as a whole was hardly affected. Due to its decentralised market economy, the United States' economy was only very marginally hit; the many other centres of economic activity, for example in Chicago, Los Angeles, Seattle or Boston, were not directly affected at all. They went on functioning without any problem. An estimated damage of 10, 20 or even 50 billion dollars is small compared to the US GNP of 10 trillion dollars. Even in Manhattan, the recovery was remarkably quick; most parts of the financial community were ready to take up work again a few days or even a few hours after the attack. This does not, of course, mean that there were no human or material losses. But the point is that even this dreadful blow was not able to seriously damage a decentralised economy like the American one. Many of the high costs were the result of the *political* response to the attack (such as grounding the entire civilian air traffic and closing down the Wall Street stock exchange), and not the result of the attack itself. Viewed from this perspective, the attack was far from being a victory to the terrorists, but rather demonstrated the strength of a decentralised economic system.

The Catholic Church with the Pope as absolute, and (in the case of church dogma) even infallible ruler, is an example of a strictly hierarchical, highly centralised organisation. Nobody can substitute for the Pope. Accordingly, the Pope presents an attractive target to terrorists and assassins alike. Indeed, there have been several known recent attempts to assassinate the Pope. To some extent, the American President with his far-reaching powers is also a worthwhile target for terrorists and assassins. The President's vulnerability is mitigated by the fact that there is a well-designed constitution exactly determining who substitutes for a President who has been assassinated. There have indeed been many attempts at assassinating American Presidents, some of which were successful. A political system with a committee of equals at the top is much less vulnerable. This is, for instance, the case in Switzerland, with its seven members of government (the *Bundesrat*), each of which has exactly the same amount of formal power. To attack one, or even several of them, would not endanger the stability of the political system.

That this system indeed works in this manner has been demonstrated by a recent incident in Switzerland. In September 2001, a man ran amok (he was not a terrorist) in the parliamentary building of the Swiss canton Zug. He shot dead no less than three of the seven members of the government council (*Regierungsrat*), as well as eleven members of parliament. He also injured a significant number of other government and parliament members. Nevertheless, within a very short period of time, the government was functional again, not least because the heads of the partly autonomous communes were able to take over.

A similar incident in Armenia plunged the country into a political crisis. In October 1999, five gunmen burst into Armenia's parliament, assassinating the Prime Minister, Parliamentary Speaker and seven other government officials. Armenia's Defence Minister stated that the situation created was fraught with uncertainty, and that the internal and external security of the state were in great danger. Because of the centralised nature of Armenia's political system, the killings left a power vacuum: there were no people at lower federal levels able to take over.

The next sections discuss polycentricity in the economy, polity, and other parts of society.

ECONOMIC DECENTRALISATION

A market economy is based on an extreme form of decentralisation of decision-making and implementation. Indeed, the advantages of the market as an efficient resources allocation mechanism break down when it is centralised via oligopolies or monopolies. Under competitive conditions, the suppliers are able to completely substitute for each other. Even if one of them is eradicated due to a terrorist attack, the other suppliers are able to fill the void immediately. They are prepared, and have an incentive, to step in. No special governmental plans have to be set up for such substitution. Of course, most economic sectors are not perfectly competitive. But as long as there is some amount of competition, there are always actual or potential suppliers who can take over. It follows that the more an economy functions according to market principles, the less vulnerable it is to terrorist attacks.

Decentralisation also contributes to avoiding and reducing the harm done by terrorist attacks in the case of monopolistic and oligopolistic sectors of the economy. Network industries, such as those for water, electricity or transportation, are less vulnerable if subunits are able to function independently.

An effective anti-terrorist policy supports economic decentralisation and competitive structures, as this greatly reduces the country's vulnerability. Obviously, an anti-terrorist policy, concentrating on decentralisation, has other attractive features: it strengthens democracy and liberalism.

POLITICAL DECENTRALISATION

Decentralising political power, or polyarchy, takes two forms.

Classical Division of Power

Political authority is distributed between a number of different political actors. Most important is the classical division of power between government, legislature and courts. Moreover, the media must be decentralised so that a terrorist attack is unable to control the flow of information. It is no accident that persons attempting a coup d'état first try to gain control over the TV broadcasting station. But if there are several TV broadcasting stations located in different places, this effort is doomed to failure. The public administration should also have at least some measure of independence, as it must be able to operate when a terrorist threat is imminent. This applies in particular to the police, the secret service and the military. Public bureaucracy is further insulated against terrorism when it itself is decentralised.

A centralised organisation invites attacks by terrorists, partly because of its functions, but also partly because of its symbolic value. Thus the planned concentration of the European Union's bureaucracy in one location in Brussels is likely to have a counterproductive effect on security. Such a building is a particularly attractive target for terrorists. While entry into the building may be less costly to control than if the offices were widely dispersed, an actual or even suspected terrorist attack causes huge costs. If, for instance, terrorists are suspected of planting a bomb in the building, work grinds to a halt because all employees have to be evacuated. This even applies for false alarms, so that the costs imposed by terrorist threats when public administration is centralised, turn out to be very substantial.

In many countries, other actors also enjoy considerable independence. Most prominent is the central bank, having the power to pursue whichever monetary policy it sees fit. But there are also regulatory authorities with a degree of independence from other political decision-makers. The reasons for such (partial) independence are based on considerations that have nothing to do with terrorism. Central bank independence has been established in many countries because it is expected that such an organisation will undertake a more long-run oriented policy than governments. The latter are (normally every four years) subject to re-election pressures, inducing them to produce short-term political business cycles in their own favour. But such a degree of independence turns out to be an effective means of lowering the vulnerability to terrorist threats. This effect is strengthened when the central bank itself is decentralised, as is the case of the American Federal Reserve, which is composed of various central banks located in a number of cities.

Spatial Decentralisation

Political power can also be divided between various levels of government. In federal (that is, spatially decentralised) countries, there are federal, state/provincial/cantonal and communal levels. In some countries, there is a fourth, regional, level between communes and provinces.

It is possible to go one step further by granting far-reaching autonomy to *f*unctional, *o*verlapping and *c*ompeting *j*urisdictions, or *FOCJ*. As each of them extends over a different area and is governed by an independent political body, this system is quite immune to terrorist attacks. Again, such jurisdictions as these have been suggested for other purposes (in this case competition between jurisdictions in order to improve the public services to the people), but their construction serves anti-terrorism policy well.

The high population density typical of large urban areas makes them ideal targets for terrorists and other aggressors. Studies (Glaeser and Shapiro, 2001) suggest indeed that there is a statistical link between terrorism and urbanisation, though they were only able to isolate a weak relationship.

The spatial decentralisation of the population is of special importance in cases where terrorists use biological and chemical weapons. In areas of highly dense population, viruses (such as smallpox) introduced by terrorists spread quickly, leading to many casualties in a short period of time. Such danger is not so great when people do not live so closely together.

Strengthening political decentralisation via the division of power and federalism contributes strongly to a country being less vulnerable to terrorist attacks. The attraction for terrorists to take aggressive action is diminished. The marginal benefits of terrorism fall and the equilibrium amount of terrorism is reduced.

A POLYCENTRIC SOCIETY

Having many centres of power can extend beyond the economy and polity. Other forms of social groups can also be more or less decentralised. There are many bodies, such as NGOs (non-governmental organisations), clubs and corporations, which are able to function in a decentralised way. Networks between firms without any hierarchical structure have become increasingly important. As the example of Linux has shown, completely decentralised open source systems are just as efficient, if not more efficient, than production of the same type of software in a hierarchical firm, such as Microsoft.

More important than the actual decentralisation of particular organisations is that many different decision-making systems should operate in a society. In a dictatorial regime, almost everything is dictated by the ruler (including which school one attends, whom one marries, which job one takes, and where one spends one's holidays), making it most vulnerable to attacks from inside and outside. In contrast, a liberal society is characterised by the coexistence of many different decision-making systems: the market, democracy, bargaining, bureaucracy and tradition. Such variety strengthens stability in case of a terrorist attack.

IS POLYCENTRICITY VIABLE?

Decentralised economic, political and other social structures have three important beneficial effects with respect to terrorist threats.

1. The target is less attractive to terrorists.
2. The units are better able to solve their problems. This makes it more unlikely that a terrorist threat arises in the first place. A good example is provided by the Alto Adige (or South Tyrol) in Italy. For many years, it was plagued by terrorist activities, which substantially hindered its economic development. In particular, tourism was negatively affected. The Italian Senate's law, according far-reaching rights of autonomy, almost certainly prevented a major eruption of terrorist violence between the Italian-speaking and German-speaking communities living in that region. Similarly, the greater degree of autonomy granted to Puerto Rico by the United States reduced political violence on the island. A study, undertaken by the World Bank (Collier and Hoeffler, 2001) for a combined cross-section and time series of 161 countries over the period from 1960 to 1999, presents indirect evidence that decentralisation may help to prevent internal violence. On the basis of 78 civil wars analysed, it is shown that strongly ethnically fractionalised, and in that respect decentralised, societies have a much lower risk of experiencing war-like internal conflicts than homogeneous societies.
3. The units are better able to react and to reorganise themselves in the event of a terrorist attack.

These are important reasons why liberal democracies in the western world have been remarkably resilient to terrorism.

Despite this, when a country is threatened with terrorism, there is an overwhelming urge to centralise decision-making powers. This tendency is particularly strong when a country has been subject to a dramatic terrorist act. The advantages of decentralisation are then completely disregarded. An example is the United States. The American mega-merger of various bodies into the new Department of Homeland Security with 169,000 employees, in this respect, is a move in the wrong direction. Any terrorist group able to attack this Department, either by the use of weapons (including biological and chemical agents) or by interfering with its electronic system, can cause considerable damage. The fact that centralising units makes them more vulnerable has been demonstrated by the two terrorist attacks on New York's twin towers. The first attack in 1993 destroyed a central command post of the police force and other support units. Nevertheless, the Mayor of New York, Rudolph Giuliani, ordered the establishment of a new central Office of Emergency Management in a building next to the World Trade Center. On September 11, 2001, this Office, which was intended to coordinate all police and support units in the event of a catastrophe, including terrorist attacks, was again destroyed and proved to be useless. Such reactions can also be observed in many other countries. When Italy and Germany faced menacing terrorist activities from the *Brigate Rosse* and the *Rote Armee Fraktion*, strongly centralised structures for anti-terrorist policy were established.

Why does such a centralising policy reaction occur, despite the fact that it may be counterproductive? Two reasons may be adduced.

1. In the case of an imminent or actual terrorist attack, the government is forced to take some quick and forceful action. Deterrence policy incorporating centralisation meets this criterion. A 'strong central command' in the short term *seems* to be an effective policy against the terrorists. In contrast, a decentralising policy takes longer to become effective. The voters on which the government in a democracy depends are less likely to attribute the positive effects of decentralisation – the lower vulnerability – to the government's actions. At best, they notice that there are fewer and less dangerous terrorist attacks than elsewhere.
2. Government politicians and public bureaucrats exploit the special situation created by terrorist threats to extend their own competencies. Having command over larger budgets and more resources increases their importance in society.

A polycentric policy is therefore not easy to achieve as a reaction to terrorism. It is a long-term strategy, having the best chances of being implemented when the terrorist danger is not imminent. It cannot be left solely to a government depending on short-run electoral success. Long-term anti-terrorist policy through decentralisation must be written into a country's constitution. The political actors – parliament, government, public bureaucracy and courts – must be given the task of guaranteeing existing polycentric structures, and expanding them wherever possible.

SUGGESTED FURTHER READING

The importance for biological systems of polycentricity, and therefore diversity to guard against outside aggression and to help stabilise systems, is discussed in:

Hirshleifer, Jack and Juan Carlos Martinez Coll (2001). 'Selection, Mutation and the Preservation of Diversity in Evolutionary Games'. In Jack Hirshleifer (ed.). *The Dark Side of the Force*. Cambridge: Cambridge University Press, pp. 251–78.

The decentralised nature of the market has been emphasised by:

Von Hayek, Friedrich A. (1978). 'Competition as Discovery Procedure'. In Friedrich A. von Hayek (ed.). *New Studies in Philosophy, Politics, Economics and the History of Ideas*. London: Routledge and Kegan Paul, pp. 119–30.

For a thorough analysis of decentralisation in all spheres of society, one of the best works is still:

Dahl, Robert A. and Charles L. Lindblom (1953). *Politics, Economics and Welfare*. New York: Harper.

Economic aspects of federalism are, for instance, treated in:

Bird, Richard M. (1986). *Federal Finance in Comparative Perspective*. Toronto: Canadian Tax Foundation.
Oates, Wallace E. (1991). *Studies in Fiscal Federalism*. Aldershot: Edward Elgar.

The concept of multiple, overlapping federal units is explored in:

Frey, Bruno S. and Reiner Eichenberger (1999). *The New Democratic Federalism for Europe: Functional Overlapping and Competing Jurisdictions*. Cheltenham, UK: Edward Elgar.

The relationship between terrorism and urbanism is the subject of:

Glaeser, Edward L. and Jesse M. Shapiro (2001). 'Cities and Warfare: The Impact of Terrorism on Urban Form'. *Journal of Urban Economics* **51**: 205–24.

Decentralised open source software production is discussed in:

Osterloh, Margit and Sandra Rota (2002). 'Open Source Software Production. The Magic Cauldron?' Mimeo, University of Zurich.

The World Bank study on the occurrence of civil wars was undertaken by:

Collier, Paul and Anke Hoeffler (2001). 'Greed and Grievance in Civil War'. Policy Research Working Paper 2355, World Bank.

The centralising tendencies of governments faced by terrorist threats are documented in:

Wilkinson, Paul (2000). *Terrorism Versus Democracy: The Liberal State Response.* London: Frank Cass.

Reducing vulnerability by avoiding exposure to terrorist threats, and reducing the harm suffered, albeit at the individual level, is also the topic of:

Keohane, Nathaniel O. and Richard J. Zeckhauser (2003). 'The Ecology of Terror Defense'. *Journal of Risk and Uncertainty* **26**(2–3): 201–229.

6. Providing Positive Incentives Not to Engage in Terrorism

POSITIVE AND NEGATIVE SANCTIONS

Basic Issues

The dominant logic in both the literature and the practice of anti-terrorism always takes 'sanctions' to be *negative*. The threat of punishment is part and parcel of deterrence policy. The intention is to dissuade actual and potential terrorists from undertaking terrorist acts, by making it clear that this involves heavy costs to them. But terrorists can also be deterred from their activities by *rewarding them* for abstaining from violent acts. In such a case, the sanctions used are *positive*.

In economic theory, positive and negative sanctions are, in principle, considered to be symmetric. Both change the opportunity set of the units sanctioned. An increase in relative costs induces those being sanctioned to systematically reduce the corresponding activity (generalised relative price effect). The symmetry is also reflected in the fact that costs are always taken to be *opportunity costs*, which means that one always compares with the next best alternative. The opportunity costs stay the same, whether a government offers terrorists a reward of a given sum of money for compliance, or threatens them with a penalty of the same amount for failure to comply. If, however, it is known that the sanctioned units react differently to rewards than to punishments (as will be argued here), it is important to maintain the distinction.

Economic policy considers both negative and positive inducements. In environmental economics, for example, both incentive taxes and incentive subsidies are proposed to make producers and consumers take into account the external (that is, non-market) effects of their activities. An increase in the cost of polluting the environment, as well as a decrease in the cost of abstaining from polluting, has beneficial effects on the natural environment. Coase's (1960) Theorem, based on establishing well-defined property rights, works with positive incentives. If the polluting firm has the property rights in clean air, the polluted firm offers it a reward to induce it to reduce the unwelcome activity. Conversely, if the polluted firm has the property rights in clean air, the polluting firm offers it compensation to tolerate some pollution.

The area most closely related to terrorism is the 'Economic Theory of Crime'. The economics of terrorism can be considered an application of this approach to a special type of illegal behaviour. This approach is based on the idea that individuals compare the benefits of a criminal act with the expected cost of punishment. They are more likely to decide against becoming criminal, the higher is the probability of being caught and the higher the expected punishment. As can be seen, the expected utility calculation of the actors subsumed focuses on *negative* sanctions, or on deterrence. The same concentration on negative sanctions can be observed in the economic analysis of tax compliance. It considers individuals' choice as lying between correctly declaring one's income (in which case one has to pay taxes) and withholding part or all of the income, but having to reckon with the chance of being caught and punished.

To summarise, the rational choice approach used in economics allows for both positive and negative sanctions, but the applications closest to issues of terrorism solely emphasise deterrence by negative sanctions. This book argues that such one-sided focus on negative sanctions is both unnecessary and damaging; indeed, positive sanctions have many important advantages.

In the international arena, positive and negative incentives have been widely used. Among the positive sanctions are granting of most-favoured-nation status; tariff reductions; debt relief; favourable taxation; access to advanced technology; military, environmental and social cooperation; security assurances; cultural exchanges; or membership in organisations. Most importantly, many of the funds dispersed as aid to countries in the Third World are given in the expectation that their faster economic development also benefits the givers. Their own export markets expand and a more peaceful world is advantageous to all. When the Soviet Union still existed, many developing countries were bribed to take sides. Today, some countries get substantial amounts of monetary support from the United States for joining the international alliance against terrorism.

Negative sanctions (already discussed in Chapter 2) range from economic boycotts to military intervention, either in response to a previous aggressive act or pre-emptively.

Differences between Positive and Negative Sanctions

There are various differences between using positive and negative rewards relevant to anti-terrorist policy. The following two are based on traditional economic reasoning.

1. The terrorists being promised a reward for reducing terrorist acts may find it advantageous to misrepresent their preferences. They have an incentive to first engage more heavily in terrorism in order to then reduce their activities to a lower level and thus receive a higher overall reward. Such *moral hazard* appears whenever the government finds it impossible to detect such strategic behaviour.
2. If terrorists are rewarded for giving up their activities, their income rises, which may make them less prepared to accept the offer. In contrast, if the government is able to punish the terrorists by imposing fines (for instance by interfering in their sources of finance), their income falls, which may make them more willing to comply with the government's demands. But such possibilities are very limited, as terrorists are financed by the underground market, which defies control by the government.

Additional asymmetries between positive and negative sanctions not considered by the rational choice approach of economics are also important. Consider first the situation of a country fighting terrorism.

-   When the government threatens punishment if terrorists pursue their activities, and terrorists comply, no further response is needed. If, however, they do not comply, the government must invest time and effort in planning its response to the terrorists' non-compliance. The use of threats provides an incentive to the sanctioning country to establish a planning process on the assumption that the terrorists will not comply. Threats of negative sanctions involve the need to plan for the worst from the very beginning and to hurt the adversary. This tends to start a vicious circle of negative interactions.

- A government attempting to induce terrorists to abstain from violent acts by promising a reward is obliged to give the reward if the terrorists do comply. The government's planning process must focus on what terrorists value. The need to think about the adversary's concerns contributes to a more beneficial attitude. This tends to start a virtuous circle of positive interactions. If the terrorists do not comply, no further response is needed. The promise of positive sanctions is accompanied by the need to give the promised reward in the event of cooperation.
- Promises impose costs on the government when it succeeds in persuading terrorists to abstain from their activities, while threats impose costs when they fail. Positive and negative sanctions are related to the probability of success in different ways. The higher the promised reward, the more likely the terrorists are to cooperate and the more likely it is that the sanctioning government has to keep its promise. This raises the cost of positive sanctions. In contrast, provided greater threats induce greater compliance (a doubtful assumption), the probability falls of having to implement the negative sanctions. This reduces the cost of heavier threats. If, however, heavier threats are ineffective, or even counterproductive (which may well be the case, as argued earlier), those threats must be implemented, causing higher costs.
- Negative sanctions (deterrence policy based on force) have become associated with characteristics such as honour, courage and masculinity (being 'macho'). Governments dependent on the short-term support of the people therefore favour them. Positive sanctions are psychologically linked to softness, weakness and lack of resolution. As long as this view is widely prevalent only governments with a high level of support from the people can engage in positive sanctions.

Consider now the asymmetries between positive and negative sanctions from the point of view of terrorists.

- Threats typically produce stress, anxiety and fear, possibly impairing terrorists' problem-solving capacity and creating resistance. They generate an impression of hostility and indifference with respect to the terrorists' concerns. A threat of high negative sanctions may make the terrorists feel cornered.

They may feel they are in an almost hopeless situation. In that situation, the relatively best response of terrorists may be to resort to very aggressive behaviour, in the hope that the high risk incurred pays off. In that case, the threats are clearly counterproductive. The situation of the terrorists is similar to a gambler in a casino who, after having lost most of his money, fears that everything is lost, except if he has the highly improbable luck to make a huge gain. He therefore puts the rest of his money on a choice with low probability but high outcome. This behaviour has been called 'gambling for resurrection' (Downs and Rocke, 1994). In contrast, when terrorists are promised a reward if they desist from future violent acts, an impression of sympathy for the concerns of terrorists is conveyed (even if the goals are not shared). Hope and reassurance are raised. Such impressions are likely to have a strong effect on the attempt to influence terrorists' behaviour.

- Positive sanctions enhance terrorists' willingness to cooperate with the government on other issues, for instance with respect to supporting the welfare of the local population or exchanging prisoners and hostages. Negative sanctions make explicit or implicit cooperation between government and terrorists in other areas more difficult, if not impossible.

- In addition to this vertical 'spillover effect', there is a long-run 'scar effect', affecting future relations. Threatening coercion reduces terrorists' willingness to have any future contact with the sanctioning government. Positive sanctions tend to invite future cooperation.

A crucial difference between positive and negative sanctions refers to the change induced in the basic form of interaction between the parties involved. If the government promises terrorists a reward for abstaining from violence, it is more probable that the terrorists will respond in similar ways. If the government uses negative sanctions, the terrorists are more likely to respond with violence. This is the message of reciprocity theory. In addition to considerable sociological and circumstantial evidence, this finding has recently been supported by careful laboratory experiments in the economic setting. While the laboratory experiments refer to individual behaviour, it does not seem too far-fetched to transfer reciprocal behaviour to the interaction between government and terrorists. But such reciprocity is by no means automatic. It may well be that positive sanctions offered by the government are (wrongly) interpreted as a sign of weakness by the terrorists, inducing them to intensify terrorist acts. However, such an interpretation is also possible in the case of negative sanctions. The terrorists may interpret threats issued by the government as a helpless gesture, underlining their weakness. As a result, the terrorists may step up their activities. In contrast, a positive approach by the government may be interpreted by the terrorists as a sign of strength, making them more willing to engage in a peaceful interaction.

Conditions for Positive Sanctions to be Successful

Can and will positive sanctions be used to overcome terrorism? Does a 'market' emerge in which governments offer a reward for abstaining from violence and terrorists respond by following a contractual obligation to abstain from their activities?

Transaction costs economics helps to answer these questions. Transaction costs theory argues that markets exist only when the costs of contracting between the agents are small. If the costs of bargaining, monitoring and implementing contracts are higher than the utility derived from the exchange, the market fails to form. Low transaction costs exist when the behaviour of the actors regarding the contract can be observed and enforced.

These basic ideas can be applied to the situation between government and terrorists. At first, the very idea of a 'contract' between government and terrorists seems naive, but such a general conclusion is premature. Indeed, reality shows that there have often been implicit and even explicit contracts between governments and terrorists. It is certainly difficult to establish contact, let alone to form a contract, between newly formed terrorist groups and the government. But the longer a terrorist group exists, the more intensive are the informal and sometimes formal contacts with the government. Often, there are special institutions serving a bridging function, among them church leaders, peace activists, international organisations and foreign governments. More demanding than establishing contact is successfully bargaining, monitoring and implementing a contract.

The contractual obligations of the government and the terrorists are difficult to observe directly. If only outcomes can be observed, there is much room for 'moral hazard'. Each side can (falsely) claim that they have followed their contractual obligations, but that the desired outcome is due to factors beyond their control. The terrorists not abstaining from terrorist acts can claim that the terrorist attacks were undertaken by other terrorist groups or by criminals. A government not coming up with the promised reward can argue that it has been prevented by parliament or by the courts. In these circumstances, the contract is undermined and becomes less and less relevant. As both the government and the terrorists rationally predict this outcome, they will not form a contract. This is market failure.

Even assuming that the behaviour of the government and the terrorist group were perfectly observable, the contract must still be *enforced*. A problem arises if the agreed exchanges do not take place simultaneously. When the government makes the first move by handing over the reward to the terrorists, the terrorists may opportunistically defect from the agreement. Conversely, the terrorist group may first fulfil the terms of the agreement (for instance by handing over their weapons), but then the government might well renege and fail to give the promised reward to the then powerless former terrorists. As both sides are rational and foresee these possible outcomes, the contract is unenforceable.

A well-defined legal framework would enable contracts to overcome the problems of lacking observability and enforcement. But the situation between the government and the terrorist group is characterised by an anarchic system, where neither party can have recourse to a higher power in enforcing the contract. But there are factors mitigating the identified problems. What is needed is that the two parties can engage in *credible commitments* to observe the terms of the contract. The following possibilities exist.

- The government and the terrorist group can voluntarily offer verifiable information about their behaviour. The terrorist groups can, for instance, invite journalists known for their objective reporting to their camps. The government can invite persons trusted by the terrorist group to monitor the behaviour of the police and army in order to ensure that they observe the agreement. Provided the exchange between the two parties is relatively good, it is possible to strike mutually beneficial bargains.
- A credible commitment can be established by taking positions imposing high costs on oneself when not following the

agreement. This separates actors capable of making credible commitments from unreliable ones. In particular, the government can publicise what obligations it has agreed to with the terrorists. If the government breaks the contract it would lose credibility within its own country and with the international community at large. The same holds for the terrorist group. But this procedure sometimes does not work. The government might argue that conditions have changed and that the promises made are therefore null and void. The terrorist group may not incur much, if any, loss of reputation if it reneges.

- The government could deposit the agreed reward with some organisation, under the condition it be paid out to the terrorists if they indeed honour the agreement. The terrorist group could deposit their arms with another country, where they remain if the government honours its obligations. If, however, the government reneges, the arms would be returned to the terrorists.

- The government and the terrorist group can also make a credible commitment to the contract by involving international organisations, which can be asked to monitor behaviour and to enforce the contract. This solution preconditions that the international organisation is considered to be neutral by both sides. The information freely offered with regard to how the two parties could conform to the contract helps to overcome mistrust. This has indeed been one of the approaches used most often to strike up and maintain a contract between the government and terrorists.

As this discussion reveals, it is difficult, but not impossible, to offer positive incentives to overcome terrorism. A whole range of options is available to ensure that implicit or explicit contracts negotiated can bear fruit. Economic analysis (Tollison and Willet, 1979) suggests that 'issue linkages' can be a successful negotiating device. It proceeds by making trade-offs explicit among issues. Mutually beneficial agreements between the government and terrorists are facilitated. To link issues is particularly important where the benefits from an agreement on a particular issue fall mainly on one side. In that case, a linkage of issues with offsetting distributional consequences helps to promote contracts, which may otherwise be impossible due to the distributional effects.

History contains many examples where rewards were offered to attain some political goal, sometimes related to terrorism. For example, in 1961, the United States provided Haiti with airport facilities worth 5 million dollars to secure its vote in the Organisation of American States to expel Cuba from the Organisation. During that period, the US was confronted with many terrorist events, often in the form of people wanting to get out of Cuba and into the United States by hijacking a plane. The US promise of billions of dollars in aid to Egypt and Israel to bring about the (now defunct) Camp David agreement is also connected to terrorism. In order to prevent the proliferation of nuclear weapons, and to safeguard them against falling into the hands of terrorists, the United States offered aid to Ukraine, Belarus and Kazakhstan. Germany agreed to pay the Soviet Union DM 50 billion in return for the withdrawal of troops from the former German Democratic Republic (Drezner, 1999–2000).

Positive sanctions do not always work in international relations. For example, President Lyndon Johnson's administration's covert offer of massive aid to North Vietnam in return for stopping the invasion of South Vietnam. The North Vietnamese government did not accept the offer, possibly because it was not backed by any credible commitment. The Reagan administration's attempt to offer arms in exchange for hostages in Iran was also not successful.

A policy of positive sanctions, instead of coercion, is often successful at the macro level. A most important instance refers to the treatment of vanquished adversaries. Many cases in history suggest that rewarding adversaries for their loyal behaviour, instead of suppressing them, is successful. The Romans practised this policy extensively. They offered conquered enemies the highly valued Roman citizenship as a reward for supporting the empire. It does not go too far to say that this beneficial approach of granting citizenship was crucial for the thousand years hegemony of the Romans (Carr, 2002). An even more important case is the treatment of Germany after the two World Wars. After World War I, the Germans (rightly) felt suppressed by the Allies. This policy was changed too late and was one of the major reasons why the National Socialist Party and other right-wing parties got so much support from the people in the late 1920s and early 1930s. The Allies completely changed their policy after World War II, despite the fact that the Nazis had committed so many more atrocities during that war. Whether this change of policy was due to a learning process, or whether it was undertaken to prevent the Soviet

Union taking over the whole European continent, remains unclear. What matters is that the United States supported Germany first with care parcels and then with large-scale aid under the Marshall Plan. Under General Douglas MacArthur, the same beneficial policy was pursued in Japan. The result was nothing short of spectacular. Both countries recovered relatively quickly from the huge devastation caused by war. They experienced a *Wirtschaftswunder* (an economic miracle), and became democratic nations committed to the rule of law and politically supporting the United States. This outcome is consistent with the notion of positive sanctions tending to improve the basic interaction between the parties involved. It speaks against the idea that terror must be answered by terror.

Opening up New Opportunities

Positive sanctions can consist of providing people with previously non-existing or unattainable opportunities to increase their utility. According to the economic terminology, the opportunity costs of being a terrorist are raised, because there are now other valued alternatives available. This formulation allows us to analyse the consequences in terms of the organising graphs presented in Chapter 4. The marginal cost curve for undertaking terrorist activities shifts upwards, as shown in Figure 4.4. The resulting equilibrium extent of terrorism is lower. The upward shift of the marginal cost curve to terrorists is the same as in the case of a coercive deterrence policy but there are no countervailing effects (as shown in Figure 4.5). When new opportunities open up for terrorists, the marginal benefit curve of committing terrorist acts stays constant, so that the equilibrium amount of terrorism is lower. One could even imagine that the marginal benefits to terrorists fall, so strengthening the equilibrium decline in terrorism. That could, for instance, be the case when terrorists are offered new opportunities in the form of better education (as discussed in the following section).

The following two sections advance concrete anti-terrorist policies based on making alternative, non-violent activities more attractive to actual and potential terrorists. These proposals suggest possibilities for enlarging valued opportunities by offering rewards *in kind* rather than directly in the form of money. Following traditional economic theory, monetary rewards are preferable to rewards in kind, because money is more fungible than goods. The recipients, in our case the terrorist groups, would be able to use the money in the best way to increase their utility. Goods received as rewards are less fungible, and are therefore less valued by the terrorists.

However, potential recipients normally reject direct money transfers in exchange for a given service. Accepting money is, in most cases, seen as a morally unacceptable bribe. Especially terrorist groups claiming to pursue some higher ideological goal (such as achieving the independence of a part of a country or freedom of religion) refuse to be openly and publicly connected with monetary payments seen as bribes. Rewards in the form of goods, though in economic terms not different in principle from money, have a less negative connotation and are preferred for that reason.

There is a close analogy to NIMBY (Not In My BackYard) projects, such as nuclear power plants, airports, waste incinerators, prisons and clinics for the physically and mentally handicapped. Such projects increase the population's overall welfare, but impose net costs on the individuals living in the host community. Although the people fully realise that these collective enterprises are desirable from the social point of view, they are not prepared to have them in their own immediate neighbourhood. There is a neat economic solution to the problem. As the aggregate net benefits of undertaking these projects are positive, one must simply redistribute them in an appropriate way. Communities which accept such a project must be compensated to make their net benefits positive; other communities and persons not affected by the project are taxed to raise the sum of compensation. In consequence, the socially beneficial project should now be accepted by the host community. The exchanges agreed are voluntary, so that everybody gains (the process leads to a *Pareto superior* outcome).

In reality, however, siting procedures, based on explicit price incentives, have rarely been successful. In the United States, for example, despite high compensation offers, the search for hazardous landfills and nuclear waste repositories offering monetary compensation proved to work only in a few, unimportant cases. In Switzerland, the offer of compensation in the form of money for accepting a nuclear waste site even led to a *reduction* in citizens' support for the project from 51 per cent to less than half, 25 per cent. The willingness to contribute to a public good was crowded out (Frey, Oberholzer-Gee and Eichenberger, 1996).

As direct monetary transfers appear to be even less appropriate in the relationship between government and terrorist groups, only rewards in non-monetary form are considered. The next section discusses improved education and its associated income opportunities, and the following section intensified social contacts and integration.

IMPROVED EDUCATION AND HIGHER INCOME

It has often been claimed that terrorism is nurtured by economic distress. The Nobel Peace Prize winners Desmund Tutu and Kim Dae Jong believe that 'at the bottom of terrorism is poverty', and Elie Wiesel and the Dalai Lama opined that 'education is the way to eliminate terrorism' (Atran, 2003: 1536). There can be little doubt that this is indeed often the case in countries of the Third World, where education and income are at a low level, and where the economic differences between the lower and upper classes are huge. The first period of Intifada (1982–88) in Palestine coincided with a sharp increase in unemployment for college graduates compared with high school graduates; the real daily wage dropped by about 30 per cent, while for those with only secondary education it remained more or less constant. Unemployment made it easier for *al Qaeda* and similar groups to recruit persons from the Arabian peninsula (Friedman, 2002).

To provide better education for the masses, and thereby better their economic opportunities, seems to be a straightforward and effective way to combat the roots of terrorism. To join a terrorist group, or even to support one, becomes a less attractive option when individuals see that they can earn a good living through legitimate work. Terrorist leaders will find it increasingly difficult to find persons prepared to engage in arduous and dangerous terrorist activities. This increase in the (opportunity) costs to terrorists brought about by offering alternative options reduces the equilibrium extent of terrorism.

However, empirical research dampens this optimistic view. In general, terrorists have above average education. Among Western and Latin American urban terrorists, such as the German *Rote Armee Fraktion* or the Italian *Brigate Rosse*, about two-thirds have some form of university education. Terrorists are recruited from widely different occupations, and no single occupation seems to produce a particularly large number of terrorists. PFLP's George Habash was a doctor of medicine, PLO's Yasser Arafat a graduate engineer, RAF's Ulrike Meinhof a journalist and Horst Mahler a lawyer. Exceptions are students and the unemployed. The latter conform to the economic expectation that persons with low opportunity costs are more willing to engage in illegal activities, including joining terrorist groups (Russell and Miller, 1977). Two reasons may be adduced as to why the number of well-educated persons is so high among terrorists.

1. Individuals with a good education find terrorism attractive, as they normally are given leadership positions at the national or at least the cell level. They can also invest (some) of their own money and thereby establish leadership. A pertinent example is Osama Bin Laden, who partly finances *al Qaeda* with funds coming from his own wealthy Saudi family. Terrorism is thus just one of many possibilities for achieving high rank and status.

2. In most cases, well-educated terrorists come from higher social classes and can hope to return to the safe haven of their family if the terrorist activities fail or if they get bored with them. Such people can better afford to yield to the notion of achieving 'good' by violence. They thus run a lower risk when engaging in terrorism than less well-connected persons.

No empirical evidence has been found that low education or poverty has any systematic effect on Palestinian, Lebanese and Israeli extremists and terrorists. This applies even to suicide bombers. Most Palestinians who have sacrificed themselves had quite a good education and are of middle-class upbringing (Krueger and Maleckovà, 2002). To assume that suicide bombers are drawn from the ranks of the impoverished, who have nothing to lose, is a wrong stereotype. Political conditions and feelings of indignity and frustration are found to be much more important reasons for individuals joining terrorist groups and committing suicide attacks than are ignorance and poverty.

The situation looks different when one considers the effect of education and economic conditions at the aggregate level. A World Bank study (Collier and Hoeffler, 2001) investigated the causes of civil war in a sample of 161 countries over the period 1960–1999. It found important effects of education and income on the 78 civil wars identified:

- a 10 per cent higher enrolment in primary school education on average reduces the likelihood of a civil war by between 9 and 12 percentage points;

- a doubling of per capita income reduces the likelihood of a civil war by 5 percentage points;
- an increase in the rate of growth of national income reduces the likelihood of a civil war by 14 percentage points.

These results refer to civil wars, but they may also be relevant for terrorism in addition to the determinants already mentioned. In some cases, there is no clear-cut difference between civil war and terrorism. These empirical results are not necessarily inconsistent with each other. It may well be that the most important effect of improved education and income occurs because a smaller number of *potential* terrorists actually join a terrorist group. But those persons who *actually* become terrorists may be relatively well educated.

Evaluation

Better education and higher income do not necessarily prevent terrorist activity. It is not possible to establish a 'stereotype' terrorist. There are many destitute and non-educated persons who never engage in terrorism. While they might have a greater tendency to engage in violence, they can become ordinary criminals. But it should also be noted that the distinction between ordinary criminals and terrorists is not well defined. Many terrorist groups, especially in Latin America (such as the Colombian FARC), are very much involved in ordinary crimes, such as extorting ransoms by taking hostages. Conversely, many terrorist leaders belong to the better-educated and richer classes of their societies. But the situation is different for the terrorist rank and file, as well as for active and passive supporters. Most importantly, an improvement in the general level of education and economic well-being reduces the number of potential terrorists in society. But this last effect is difficult to gauge, as it is uncertain what might have happened if the educational and income changes had not taken place.

Taking these reservations into account, the following conclusions can be drawn.

- Improving education and raising income is an effective anti-terrorism strategy in the long term and in countries of the Third World with widespread social inequalities.
- This policy does not prevent particular individuals engaging

in terrorism, especially intellectuals or religiously motivated persons.

- The policy works indirectly by reducing the number of persons potentially engaging in terrorism.

As improving education and income are certainly not sufficient to overcome terrorism, the next section considers a more direct approach to opening up new opportunities in an attempt to discourage people from engaging in terrorism.

INTENSIFYING SOCIAL CONTACTS AND SOCIAL INTEGRATION

Reintegrating Terrorists

One of the most fundamental of human motivations is the need to belong. People want to form and maintain lasting positive and significant interpersonal relationships. This also applies to terrorists. As long as they belong to a terrorist group, their sense of belonging is fulfilled. In most cases, former relationships with the family, friends and acquaintances are completely severed when they join a terrorist group. The same tends to happen when people join an extremist religious sect. In some cases, as with Islamic terrorist groups, both go together. The isolation from other social entities gives strength to the terrorist group, because it has become the only place where the sense of belonging is nurtured. Terrorist leaders employ this need to belong by closely binding individual members into small terrorist cells. People typically rely on sources of authority because of the high cost of discovering and verifying every bit of knowledge for themselves. Extremist views are therefore more likely to flourish in isolated groups of like-minded people. This is a generally recognised fact revealed in research on religious sects. Moreover, extreme views serve as norms of exclusion. Extremism therefore reinforces segregation and vice versa. Terrorist leaders can be seen as entrepreneurs exploiting and magnifying the differences between the isolated groups. They 'supply hatred' as this furthers their political aims. It makes the terrorist leaders' often taxing demands on the ordinary members more appealing to them.

An effective way to overcome terrorism is to break up this isolation.

Interaction between groups tends to reduce extremist views (Takács, 2001). Stopping the vicious circle of segregation and extremism can be expected to lower terrorists' inclination to participate in violent activities. The terrorists need to experience that there are other social bodies able to give them a sense of belonging. If that can be achieved, the power of the terrorist leaders over its members is reduced, because individuals become aware that preferable alternatives to terrorism exist.

There is strong evidence from experimental research in game theory that communication and personal contacts between players increases cooperation. A meta-analysis of hundreds of social-dilemma experiments concludes that 'the experimental evidence shows quite clearly that discussion has an extremely positive effect on subjects' willingness to cooperate' (Sally, 1995: 61; see also Bohnet and Frey, 1999). Sociological studies for various countries affected by terrorism, such as Ireland, the Basque country and Israel, indicate that social segregation is to a great extent responsible for repeated ethnic conflict.

Offering terrorists a new sense of belonging reduces the social isolation brought about by their membership in a cell or group. This is not easy to achieve, as the terrorist leaders try to prevent all social contacts not sanctioned by them. It is therefore important that the few 'unofficial' contacts a terrorist may have are used to loosen the ties with the terrorist group. An important condition is that the contacts established are characterised by procedural fairness. Consistency, objectivity and correctness are instrumental in guiding the relationship of the government and other actors with the individual terrorists. There must also be interactive fairness; each terrorist needs to be treated with respect. An anti-terrorist policy of overcoming the social exclusion of the terrorists may appear to be ineffective in the short run. But it promises to lead to the best possible outcome for all parties involved in the medium and long term.

In many cases, the representatives of the government and its agencies (police and army) are unable to behave in such a way as to overcome terrorists' social isolation. They tend to see terrorists as deadly enemies to be eliminated. Often they have a personal grudge against the terrorists, because they themselves have suffered personal losses (for instance friends in uniform may have been killed by the terrorist group). But for the anti-terrorist policy to be successful, the reigning principle must be whether the social isolation of the terrorist can be broken and therefore the terrorist threat undermined. To follow a thirst for revenge drives the terrorists back into isolation. This would conform exactly to the wishes of the terrorist leaders. They are well aware that their group's cohesiveness is undermined if they are no longer able to control the social contacts of individual members. Interestingly enough, the terrorist leaders and the staunch supporters of a deterrence approach share a common goal in this respect.

There are various ways to motivate terrorists to interact more closely with other members of society and to thereby overcome their isolation.

- The terrorists can be involved in a *discussion process*, which takes their goals and grievances seriously and which tries to see whether compromises are feasible. Moreover, terrorists can be granted access to the normal political process. This lowers the costs of pursuing the political goal by legal means and hence raises the opportunity costs of terrorism. This is no utopian solution. In the Netherlands, for example, terrorist sympathisers are granted access to the media to a considerable extent (Chalk, 1995). As a consequence, they do not have to turn to illegal means, and possibly bloodshed, in order to communicate their views. This does not mean, however, that TV viewers would be convinced by their arguments, or even become more favourably inclined towards their ideologies (see, more fully, Chapter 7).

- The terrorists, and in particular their supporters and sympathisers, can be involved in the institutionalised political process. An example is provided by a terrorist campaign in Switzerland, ending with a direct democratic decision on the disputed issue (Rom, 2000). A separatist movement in the remote northern districts of the Bernese Jura demanded secession from the Canton Berne. Because of an uncompromising attitude on the part of the Bernese government, the conflict escalated. In the 1960s, the *Front de libération jurassien* (Jurassian Liberation Front) and the *Béliers* (Battering Rams) were formed. They were responsible for a number of incendiary attacks and bombings. It was only after the Bernese government decided that the electorate of the Bernese Jura should determine its own political future that the conflict de-escalated. A popular referendum, which was preceded by intensive public discussion, led to the establishment of a new canton. In subsequent referenda, some communes and districts voted in favour of remaining part of Canton Berne. The *Front de libération jurassien* and the *Béliers* continued their attacks, with the objective of a unification of all the districts. However, they lost popular support and soon ceased to exist. In contrast, to exclude terrorist sympathisers from the political process is likely to be counterproductive. This applies, for instance, to the Spanish government's ban of the political wing *Herri Batasuna* of the Basque terrorist organisation ETA.

The same principle of anti-terrorist policy can be applied to nations supporting or harbouring terrorists. If such countries are internationally isolated and identified as 'rogue states', they tend to become more extreme and ideological. A more fruitful strategy is to help them to re-enter the international community and to honour its rules. Only then is it possible to form an encompassing international coalition among states against terrorism. The crucial importance of securing the cooperation of as many states as possible has been a major topic of the research on terrorism.

Welcoming Repentants

Persons engaged in terrorist movements can be offered incentives, most importantly reduced punishment and a secure future, if they are prepared to leave the organisation they are involved with and are ready to talk about it and its objectives. Terrorists who credibly show that they wish to renounce terrorist activities should be supported and not penalised. The prospect of being supported raises a member's opportunity costs of remaining a terrorist. Such an approach has indeed been used in practice with great success. Examples are the *Brigate Rosse* in Italy, the *Rote Armee Fraktion* in Germany and the *Action Directe* in France. In Italy, a law introduced in 1982, the *legge sui pentiti* (law on repentants), left it up to the discretion of the courts to reduce sentences quite substantially, on condition that convicted terrorists provide tangible information leading to the arrest and conviction of fellow terrorists. Convicted terrorists, both in Germany and Italy, received reduced prison sentences and other concessions, even including daytime furloughs from prison in order to be able to hold down a normal job. Serious terrorist crimes were effectively depenalised through offering terrorists the chance to resign, admit their guilt and inform on other terrorists. The implementation of this principal witness programme turned out to be an overwhelming success (Taylor and Quayle, 1994; Wilkinson, 2000). It provided the police with detailed information, which helped to crack open the *Brigate Rosse* cells and columns and enabled former terrorists to return to normal life again.

Offering Valued Opportunities

Persons inclined to follow terrorist ideas and undertake terrorist actions can be invited to visit foreign countries. Universities and research institutes, for example, can offer such persons the opportunity to discuss their ideology with intellectuals. The guests may, moreover, pursue their own studies. It is to be expected that confrontation with the liberal ideas existing in such places of learning will mellow their terrorist inclinations. The very least which would be achieved is that the (potential) terrorists have access to new and radically different ideas, compared with the situation in which they live within a closed circle of other terrorists.

EVALUATION

Providing positive incentives to terrorists for ceasing to engage in violent actions represents a completely different approach from the conventional anti-terrorist policy of deterrence. A conscious effort is made to break the organisational and mental dependence of persons on the terrorist organisations by offering them more favourable alternatives. Deterrence policy does the opposite: the costs of remaining a terrorist are raised.

The policy of opening up alternatives to the terrorists is not ideal. It has some disadvantages, but also strong advantages. Both are discussed in the following section.

Disadvantages

There are four major weaknesses in the effort to raise terrorists' opportunity costs and to thereby reduce the incidence of terrorism. However, some of them are imaginary rather than real.

- The strategy may not work because the incentives created are insufficient to attract terrorists. This may be especially true for strongly intrinsically motivated or fanatical terrorists. The incentives are likely to be ineffective in diverting the hard core of terrorist organisations from participating in illegal activities. To be effective, the strategy would require extremely large positive incentives and would entail considerable costs. They may prove successful in restraining the *Umfeld* (environment or periphery) of the terrorists from terrorist activities. But all terrorist movements rely on the support of the *Umfeld*. Without it, the hard core of the terrorist organisations would only be able to undertake low-scale terrorist activities.

- The leaders of the terrorist movements may try to undermine the positive approach by undertaking a counter-strategy (for example by offering similarly appreciated alternatives or by threatening punishment). They can also act strategically; for example, by sending some trusted members as 'principal witnesses', and therefore misleading the police. But such counter-strategies are costly for the terrorist movement and may be detected by the anti-terror forces.

- The positive approach may create perverse incentives, similar to the 'moral hazard' mentioned at the beginning of this chapter. Rational actors, anticipating the ease of exit, are more inclined to enter in the first place. This is a common argument in the discussion of drug policies. However, there is no empirical evidence that ease of exit induces more entry into terrorist organisations.

- The strategy may be considered immoral and therefore be rejected. It may be thought that the terrorists are rewarded for their illegal and often heinous acts. But it could be argued that it is much better that the persons concerned stop being terrorists, and no longer produce the heavy costs associated with such activities. It should be kept in mind that there are many cases in which 'terrorists' have later been fully integrated into society. Some of these people achieved high political ranks and a few of them were even awarded the Nobel Prize for Peace. To name only the most prominent examples: Menachem Begin, one of the principal leaders of *Irgun Zvai Leumi* (National Military Organisation), later Prime Minister of Israel and 1978 Nobel Peace Prize laureate; his successor as prime minister, Yizhak Shamir, formerly principal director of operations of the *Lohamei Herut Yisrael* (Freedom Fighters of Israel); Ahmed

Ben Bela and Houari Boumedienne, founding members of the *Front de Libération Nationale* (National Liberation Front) and presidents of Algeria from 1963 to 1965 and 1968 to 1978 respectively; George Grivas, leader of the *Ethniki Organosis Kypriakou Agonos* (National Organisation of Cypriot Fighters) and later in charge of the Greek forces in Cyprus; Nelson Mandela, founder of the *Umkhonto we Sizwe* (Spear of the Nation), 1993 Nobel Peace Prize laureate and president of South Africa; Yasser Arafat, founding member of the *Al Fatah* (Victory), 1994 Nobel Peace Prize laureate and president of the Palestinian council governing the West Bank and Gaza Strip; Gerry Adams, president of *Sinn Féin* (We Ourselves) and allegedly a former holder of a number of senior positions within the Irish Republican Army; Martin McGuinness, leader of the Irish Republican Army at the time of Bloody Sunday 1972 and former deputy head of *Sinn Féin*; and Billy Hutchinson and David Erskine, former members of the Ulster Volunteer Force and currently members of the Progressive Unionist Party in Ireland (Frey and Luechinger, 2003a).

Strengths

There are two crucial advantages in the strategy of offering alternatives to terrorists.

- The whole interaction between terrorists and government takes the character of a *positive sum game*. Everybody benefits. The efforts of the government are no longer aimed at destruction. Rather, the government makes an effort to raise the utility of those terrorists who choose to enter the programmes offered. This interaction – even if many terrorists do not participate – has a better chance of producing a Pareto-superior outcome. In contrast, deterrence policy unavoidably produces a worse situation for both sides. The terrorists are punished (incarcerated, killed, etc.), while the government often has to raise large sums of money to undertake their deterrence strategy. The negative interaction between the Palestinian terrorists and the Israeli government provides a good illustration. There can be no doubt that both sides are worse off as a result of this vicious circle.

- The strategy *undermines the cohesiveness of the terrorist organisation*. The incentive to leave is a strong threat to the organisation. The terrorist leaders no longer know whom to trust because, after all, most persons can succumb to temptation. An effort to counteract these temptations, by prohibiting members from having any contact outside the terrorist camp and from taking up the attractive offers, leads to conflicts between leaders and rank and file. When good outside offers are available to the members, the leaders tend to lose control. The terrorist organisation's effectiveness is thereby reduced.

The discussion reveals that the positive approach to dealing with terrorism has some weaknesses. But several of them are more apparent than real. Compared with the major advantages of the positive approach, one may conclude that the respective anti-terrorist policies would be beneficial and should be undertaken.

SUGGESTED FURTHER READING

The role of positive and negative incentives in economics is discussed in:

Frey, Bruno S. (1999). *Economics as a Science of Human Behaviour.* Boston, Dordrecht and London: Kluwer.

For the economic theory of crime, see:

Becker, Gary S. (1968). 'Crime and Punishment: An Economic Approach'. *Journal of Political Economy* **76** (2): 169–217.
Cameron, Samuel (1988). 'The Economics of Crime Deterrence: A Survey of Theory and Evidence'. *Kyklos* **41**: 301–23.

A survey on the economic approach to tax evasion is given in:

Andreoni, James, Brian Erard and Jonathan Feinstein (1998). 'Tax Compliance'. *Journal of Economic Literature* **76**: 818–60.

Important early contributions to the possibilities and limits of positive sanctions in international relations are due to:

Baldwin, David A. (1971). 'The Power of Positive Sanctions'. *World Politics* **24** (1): 19–38.
Galtung, Johan (1965). 'On the Meaning of Nonviolence'. *Journal of Peace Research* **2** (3): 228–57.

Hirschman, Albert O. (1964). 'The Stability of Neutralism: A Geometrical Note'. *American Economic Review* **54** (2): 94–100.

See also:

Frey, Bruno S. (1984). *International Political Economics*. Oxford: Blackwell.

More recent works on the use of economic incentives in international politics are:

Baldwin, David A. (1985). *Economic Statecraft*. Princeton, NJ: Princeton University Press.
Bernauer, Thomas and Dieter Ruloff (eds) (1999). *The Politics of Positive Incentives in Arms Control*. Columbia, SC: University of South Carolina Press.
Drezner, Daniel W. (1999). *The Sanctions Paradox. Economic Statecraft and International Relations*. Cambridge: Cambridge University Press.
Cortright, David (1997). *The Price of Peace. Incentives and International Conflict Prevention*. Lanham, MD: Rowman & Littlefield.

The observation that opponents tend to respond in similar terms, and that reciprocal behaviour is important, has long been understood in psychology and sociology. The effect has recently been studied in economics, mainly in laboratory experiments by:

Fehr, Ernst and Simon Gächter (1998). 'Reciprocity and Economics. The Economic Implications of Homo Reciprocans'. *European Economic Review* **42**: 845–59.
Fehr, Ernst, Urs Fischbacher and Simon Gächter (2002). 'Strong Reciprocity, Human Cooperation and the Enforcement of Social Norms'. *Human Nature* **13**: 1–25.

The transactions costs approach is due to:

Coase, Ronald (1988). *The Firm, the Market, and the Law*. Chicago: Chicago University Press.
Williamson, Oliver E. (1985). *The Economic Institutions of Capitalism. Firms, Markets, Relational Contradicting*. New York: Free Press.

For the role of credible commitments to solve international conflicts, see:

Schelling, Thomas C. (1960). *The Strategy of Conflict*. Oxford: Oxford University Press.

The NIMBY (Not In My BackYard) problem is discussed in:

Portney, Kent E. (1991). *Siting Hazardous Waste Treatment Facilities: The NIMBY Syndrome*. New York: Auburn House.

The crowding-out effect connected with offering monetary compensation is more generally treated in:

Frey, Bruno S. (1997). *Not Just for the Money.* Cheltenham, UK and Brookfield, USA: Edward Elgar.

The role of terrorists' education is discussed in:

Russell, Charles and Bowman H. Miller (1977). 'Profile of a Terrorist'. *Terrorism: An International Journal* **1** (1): 17–34.

The central importance of belonging as a human motivation is treated, for instance, in:

Baumeister, Roy F. and Mark R. Leary (1995). 'The Need to Belong: Desire for Interpersonal Attachments as a Fundamental Human Motivation'. *Psychological Bulletin* **117** (3): 497–529.
Van Beest, Ilja, Henk Wilke and Eric van Dijk (2004). 'The Interplay of Self-interest and Equity in Coalition Formation'. *European Journal of Social Psychology*, forthcoming.

That personal interactions reduce extremism is put forward, among others, by:

Hardin, Russel (2002). 'The Crippled Epistemology of Extremism'. In Albert Breton, Gianluigi Galeotti, Pierre Salmon and Ronald Wintrobe (eds). *Political Extremism and Rationality.* New York: Cambridge University Press, pp. 3–22.
Breton, Albert and Silvana Dalmazzone (2002). 'Information Control, Loss of Autonomy, and the Emergence of Political Extremism'. In Albert Breton, Gianluigi Galeotti, Pierre Salmon and Ronald Wintrobe (eds). *Political Extremism and Rationality.* New York: Cambridge University Press, pp. 44–66.

Another valuable recent contribution is by:

Glaeser, Edward L. (2002). 'The Political Economy of Hatred'. NBER Working Paper No. 9171, Cambridge, MA: National Bureau of Economic Research.

The great importance of the international cooperation of countries in fighting terrorism is extensively described in:

Byman, Daniel L. and Matthew C. Waxman (2002). *The Dynamics of Coercion. American Foreign Policy and the Limits of Military Power.* Cambridge: Cambridge University Press.
Sandler, Todd and Walter Enders (2004). 'An Economic Perspective on Transnational Terrorism'. *European Journal of Political Economy*, forthcoming.

That ease of exit does not necessarily increase entry is demonstrated in the case of drugs in:

Miron, Jeffrey A. and Jeffrey Zweifel (1995). 'The Economic Case Against Drug Prohibition'. *Journal of Economic Perspectives* **9** (4): 175–92.

7. Diffusing Media Attention

TERRORISM AND THE MEDIA

Extensive Coverage

Our discussion has so far focused on anti-terrorism policies over the medium and long term. The proposals to decentralise society and to raise education and income require considerable time to implement and are not quick to bear fruit. To offer positive incentives to terrorists by intensifying social contacts and integration is more of a proposal for the medium term than one to be applied immediately.

This chapter proposes an anti-terrorist policy that is relevant once a terrorist attack has taken place. It is especially directed at major and spectacular events, such as the kidnapping of famous persons. Spectacular terrorist incidents are closely linked to media coverage, in particular television. The proposal therefore seeks to reduce terrorist violence by influencing media reporting. But the proposal suggests a rather unconventional procedure for reaching this goal.

The relationship between terrorists and the media has received considerable attention in the literature. It can be described as 'symbiotic', with the interests of the terrorists being in one respect similar, or even identical, to those of the media. Both want to make news, and both want to keep the incident in the headlines for as long as possible. Some authors have gone so far as to claim that there would be no terrorism without the media. Think about these statements:

- If the media were not there to report terrorist acts and to explain their political and social significance (the motives inspiring them and so forth), terrorism as such would cease to exist. (O'Sullivan, 1986: 70); or
- The success of a terrorist operation depends almost entirely on the amount of media publicity it gets. (Laqueur, 1977: 109).

It is therefore necessary to consider a third group of actors in addition to the terrorists and the government, namely the media: journalists reporting (actual or invented events), anchor persons massaging the news, and editors seeking a wide coverage by newspapers, radio and, most importantly, television. As is the case for terrorists and the government, the media are far from being a unitary actor. Indeed, one of their major characteristics is the intense competition between the various suppliers. There are even media prominent the world over solely because of their special coverage of terrorist activities. *Aljazeera* is a pertinent example, due to its special access to some major terrorists, in particular Osama Bin Laden. Television today provides a forum for the political struggle between terrorists and governments.

Dramatic terrorist actions receive huge media attention. An example is the coverage of the skyjacking of TWA flight 847 by the Lebanese *Shi'a* terrorists (a part of *Hezbollah*) en route from Rome to Cairo in June 1985. They demanded the release of over 750 *Shi'a* held in Israeli prisons. The kidnapped plane was first flown to Beirut, then to Algiers, then back to Beirut. At each stop, non-American passengers, as well as women and children, were released, with 39 American men remaining in the terrorists' hands. During the 17-day drama, on average 14 out of 21 minutes of the daily early evening 'flagship' news were devoted to the hostage story. When the 39 hostages were finally released, the network coverage of the event by all three nationwide US networks (CBS, ABC and NBC) came close to nearly 100 per cent (Crelinsten, 1990). This means that *no* other event in the world was deemed to be as important as the proceedings surrounding the release of those hostages.

Other terrorist activities able to capture a large part of media attention, especially in the United States include, for instance, the 444-day siege with hostages at the US Embassy in Teheran in 1979–80. Similar huge media attention also occurred when other countries were affected by spectacular terrorist acts, such as in Germany the kidnapping and execution of the president of the *Deutsche Arbeitgebervereinigung*, Hanns Martin Schleyer, in 1977, or in Italy of the former prime minister, Aldo Moro, in 1978. During the 55-day crisis in Italy, only two articles on the front pages of the country's newspapers had no connection with this terrorist incident (Crelinsten, 1990).

The most impressive example is September 11, 2001. The attacks on the World Trade Center towers and the Pentagon, and the subsequent collapse of the twin towers within two and a half hours, were captured on film and relayed to billions of TV viewers worldwide. The event *completely* dominated the American news for a full week, and not even advertising (on whose revenue the TV stations live) was allowed to interfere.

The huge media attention devoted to spectacular terrorist events has been made possible by two recent technological advances on the supply side facilitating television broadcasting. In 1968, the first television satellite enabled transmission from virtually any place in the world. In the early 1970s, the portable lightweight video-recording camera made live television transmissions possible. This means that the TV viewer is placed at the very scene of the terrorist act, and in this sense is a part of it.

On the demand side, the nearly complete coverage of all households in developed economies (often with several TV sets), and its rapid expansion in countries of the Second and Third World, enables a worldwide audience to be tapped. TV has become a main source of information and entertainment in all countries. By 1978, television had become the *only* source of news for one third of Americans. For two-thirds of Americans, it constitutes the main source. Modern TV news tends to be more rapid than the information provided by the secret service. It is therefore not surprising that when a major terrorist attack takes place, politicians and public officials follow its course on commercial and public TV stations. It has even been quipped that 'CNN (a commercial station) runs ten minutes ahead of NSA (the super-secret electronic signals gathering American intelligence agency)' (quoted in Hoffman, 1998: 151). This was also true during the dramatic hours of September 11, 2001.

Terrorists Exploit the Media

Terrorists have become very skilled in using the media to achieve maximum publicity. They have learned what the media need to propagate their political demands to millions and even billions of people. Several aspects are important:

- Terrorism has become a sort of theatrical drama, or perverted form of show business, in which the terrorists often orchestrate their attacks in order to attain maximum attention.
- The major TV channels invest vast amounts of resources in covering spectacular terrorist attacks. In the case of the skyjacking

of TWA flight 847, within days a total of 85 employees of the three national TV networks were assembled in Beirut (Hoffman, 1998). To justify the subsequent substantial expenses, the media shared a common interest with the terrorists: to ensure the longevity of the 'story'. The journalists are pressed to blow up, and partly invent, incidents of potential interest to the viewers. This multiplies the effect of a particular terrorist act.

This discussion shows the intimate link between terrorists and the media. But governments dealing with terrorists also have the opportunity to influence media reporting in their favour. A police or military attack on terrorists, for example, certainly also constitutes news and will be widely reported.

EFFECTS OF MEDIA COVERAGE

Induced Changes in Behaviour

Technological advances, especially in TV reporting, have had systematic effects on terrorists' behaviour. The marginal benefits of undertaking terrorist acts have increased. While Figure 4.6 depicts a downward shift, the technological developments have led to an *upward* shift of the marginal benefit curve. This has raised the equilibrium extent and intensity of terrorism. Due to TV attention, terrorists are becoming skilled at creating acts especially for that medium. Taken to its extreme, TV then not only reports news, but the news takes place because the media want to cover it. The step to 'chequebook' journalism is small. This can be seen as a *reversion of causality*. It is especially critical when the terrorist acts involve large-scale violence, brutality and casualties. This is the rule rather than the exception, because otherwise TV reporters show little interest in covering the incident.

In other words, terrorists have started to change their tactics in order to accommodate media needs. This is one of the major reasons why Latin American, North African and Arab terrorists have shifted their activities from the rural to the urban areas. In cities, especially in capitals, terrorists can always count on the presence of reporters and TV cameras. To kill a dozen persons in a remote village is scarcely noted by the media, while the same violence is big news in the capital.

Predictably, terrorists mainly kidnap nationals from countries with large TV stations able to afford complete coverage of the event. Taking Americans as hostages guarantees a much larger media reaction than for any other country. Americans have therefore been kidnapped more often.

There is also quite a different behavioural effect on terrorists. Terrorists profit from the news reported. They are often well informed about the intended actions of the government and can adjust their tactics accordingly. In this regard, direct coverage supports terrorist activities.

News may also have a big impact on government policy. In the case of kidnapping, reporting puts pressure on the government, because the TV journalists, in need of material to broadcast, focus on the distraught family members of the victims, who want the government to yield to the terrorists' demands. In contrast, more general aspects of anti-terrorism policy are disregarded. This indeed happened in the TWA flight 847 hostage event. The Reagan administration was forced by intense domestic pressure to compel Israel to release 756 imprisoned *Shi'a* members in return for the 39 American hostages.

Effects on Media Consumers

The importance given in the media to terrorist activities tends to distort people's perceptions about the dangers of terrorism. They are greatly overestimated. A study by RAND, a US think tank, (see Hoffman, 1998) found that, in 1989, 14 per cent of Americans believed that, when flying, they were likely to be skyjacked or blown up by a bomb smuggled onto a plane by terrorists. In actual fact, the probability was just 0.001 per cent for skyjackings (no data are available for bombs placed on board aircraft). A comparison to road accidents is also revealing. In the same year, 45,582 persons were killed in automobile accidents in the United States while 23 lost their lives in terrorist attacks throughout the world. A year earlier, in 1988, the ratio was 47,087 to 203 (93 per cent of whom were in one event, the in-flight bombing over Lockerbie). The dramatic terrorist attack of September 11, 2001 cost the lives of about 3000 persons. This is still a relatively small number compared with other causes of death. It can, of course, not be excluded that ratios could change considerably in the future, in particular if terrorists are able to use biological, chemical or nuclear weapons of mass destruction. But this is not the issue here, for we are discussing how the extensive media coverage of terrorist acts leads to a systematic overestimation of the rate of occurrence.

Media consumers are obviously fascinated by reports on terrorism, especially when they can follow the events live: It is an extreme case of 'reality TV', which is generally very popular. But fascination is not the same as support or even understanding. No evidence has been found that the media coverage has had any effect on media consumers' attitudes towards terrorism. Despite the fact that terrorists have received such a huge amount of attention, and have sometimes even been able to state their case in front of cameras, TV viewers have not changed their negative opinions about terrorism in general, or of particular terrorist movements (Wilkinson, 2000). This is important, as attitudes or opinions affect behaviour in low-cost decisions, most importantly in voting. There is no reason to assume that voters have become more tolerant of terrorism due to their media exposure.

It can be concluded that the media exert considerable influence through their reporting on terrorism. Media, in particular TV, reporting systematically influences the behaviour of both terrorists and governments. Even if it has no effect on TV viewers' opinions, governments have long sought ways and means to control the media's stance towards terrorist events.

CONTROLLING THE MEDIA

There are three possible approaches to influencing the media's reporting on terrorism.

Voluntary Agreements

The media industry is aware of the potentially enhancing effect it can have on terrorism and can try to bind itself by forming voluntary agreements. The industry specifies rules of acceptable behaviour, forbidding, for instance, that terrorists are paid for their statements in front of the camera. It is also unacceptable that countermoves by the government are revealed to the terrorists. The media may rationally seek such conventions in order to avoid the possibility of government actions restraining them even more.

The first problem is that it is difficult, if not impossible, to make all relevant TV stations join the voluntary agreement. While it seems feasible for the major national networks in the United States, it is far more difficult to induce TV stations located in other countries to join.

A second major problem with this approach is the strong competition between the media networks. The situation corresponds to a classical Prisoner's Dilemma. All the actors agree that the media should not support terrorism. But each actor reaps large benefits, in terms of viewer interest, when breaking the agreement, and reporting a 'hot' story. In each particular case the perpetrator can always argue that the viewers wanted to see the story, that they have a 'right' to see it. A station that has a 'hot' terrorist story, but does not use it, runs the risk that other stations are less strict about adhering to the rules and show it. The viewers willingly devour the interesting news, and the station reneging the agreement greatly benefits from the massive increase in its audience.

Censorship

The government can directly intervene to enforce an acceptable mode of behaviour by the media. Several democratic Western governments have followed this course. The British government, under Margaret Thatcher, prohibited the media from allowing representatives of the Irish Republican Army and its political arm, *Sinn Féin*, to broadcast their ideology. This prohibition was later revoked. The Irish Republic also banned interviews with Ulster terrorists. In 1976, the Federal Republic of Germany made it an offence to encourage, or to publicly advocate, undermining the stability of the state, an act targeted at the media's handling of terrorists.

Fighting terrorism through censorship has the cost of restricting the freedom of the media. In the name of fighting terrorism, a fundamental democratic right is endangered. This is all the more serious, as there are always ways to circumvent the restrictions imposed. In Britain, for instance, the TV news programmes used actors to speak on screen in lieu of the *Sinn Féin* leaders.

As is the case with voluntary agreements, it seems impossible to force the TV stations outside of one's own country to comply with the censorship. Many of the media located in one of over 150 nations in the world would willingly seize the opportunity to report on terrorist events, as people are eager to consume such news. Due to the intense competition in the media industry, the media in other countries are compelled to follow.

No Intervention

Democratic governmental decision-makers, and possibly the courts appealed to when balancing the costs and benefits of government intervention, may decide not to interfere in the media's activities. Although one reason may be the constitutionally guaranteed freedom of the media, more important is the media competition on an international scale. The only super-power existing today, the United States, often tries to enforce its laws outside the US. Where controlling the media is concerned, this will almost certainly fail, except perhaps in the very short run. The incentive for a particular news agency to come up with 'hot' news, and thereby find a large audience, is too strong. Moreover, in the age of mobile phones and e-mail, an effort to suppress information cannot work. News on terrorism of interest to media consumers will always find its way to those consumers. As the decision-makers are well aware of these possibilities, they are rational in not attempting to intervene in the media's reporting on terrorism.

The discussion has shown that attempts to establish voluntary agreements or impose censorship will not work. Is non-intervention then the only option? But that would mean that the negative effects of the interaction between the media and terrorists described here would have to be tolerated. The next section proposes quite a different anti-terrorist media policy. It is not undermined by the competition among the media, nor does it passively accept the negative effects of the media with respect to terrorism.

REDUCING MEDIA ATTENTION BY SUPPLYING MORE INFORMATION

Many Terrorist Groups May be Responsible

Terrorists can be prevented from committing violent acts if they benefit less from them. This corresponds to a downward shift of the marginal benefit curve to terrorists, as shown in Figure 4.6. As a result, the equilibrium extent of terrorism will decrease.

A specific way to ensure that terrorists derive lower benefits from terrorism consists in the government ascertaining that a particular terrorist act is *not attributed to a particular terrorist group*. This prevents terrorists receiving credit for the act and thereby gaining full public attention for having committed it. The government must see to it that no particular terrorist group is able to monopolise media attention. There are two strategies for preventing such a situation arising.

- All information on who committed a particular terrorist act is *suppressed*. But in an open and free society, it is impossible to withhold the type of information that the public is eager to know. As has been discussed, the freedom of the press is seriously limited either by 'voluntary' agreement or by censorship. Such intervention does not bind the foreign press and news media. Any news about the occurrence of a terrorist act and the likely perpetrators is therefore very likely to leak out. The terrorists can easily inform foreign news agencies who, due to the competitive pressure to provide interesting news, will normally be ready to inform the world at large about the terrorist act. This first strategy must therefore be rejected as being ineffective and incompatible with democracy.
- Media attention may be *dispersed* by supplying *more* information to the public than desired by perpetrators of a particular violent act. This can be done by making it known that several terrorist groups could be responsible for a particular terrorist act. The authorities have to reveal that they never know with absolute certainty which terrorist group may have committed a violent act. Even when it seems obvious which terrorist group is involved, the police can never be sure. The terrorist act may even have been committed by a politically opposed group. It may have undertaken the act in order to incriminate the more 'obvious' groups, and invite police action against the latter. Rather, it is only fair that the government publicly discuss various reasonable hypotheses. They have to refrain from attributing a terrorist act with any degree of certainty to a particular group, as long as the truth is not established. In a lawful country, based on the division of power, this is the privilege of the courts, but not of the executive branch.

In the case of many spectacular, and therefore newsworthy, terrorist events, *no* credible claims by the perpetrators have ever been made (Lesser et al., 1999: 27–8). These events include some of the most important terrorist attacks:

- the sarin nerve-gas attack in Tokyo (1995);
- the bombing of the Federal Office Building in Oklahoma City (1995);
- the car bombings in Bombay killing 317 persons (1993);
- the bomb destroying the Jewish community centre in Buenos Aires, killing 96 persons (1994);
- the in-flight bombing of Pan Am flight 103, killing 278 persons (1988).

In most of these terrorist attacks, the perpetrators were later identified and are known today. But such knowledge did *not* exist when the event happened. At that time, many different terrorist groups, or even a combination of them, might have been credible aggressors.

In many cases, however, several groups claim to have committed a particular terrorist act. For example, in the terrorist attack on the discotheque 'La Belle' in Berlin in 1986, the Anti-American Arab Liberation Front, the Red Army Faction, RAF, and an offshoot of the RAF, the Holger Meins Commando, all claimed responsibility for the blast. But the media are often quick to attribute an attack to some innocent terrorist group, as it later turned out (Laqueur, 1977: 106).

The government has to stress that any one of the groups claiming responsibility *may* be the one responsible. As a consequence, the media disperse the public's attention to many different, and possibly conflicting, political groups and goals. When only one group claims to have committed the terrorist act, the authorities responsible have to point out that such a claim is not substantiated. Indeed, experience shows that several different groups may have undertaken the act, but choose to remain silent. The government may point out that many cases are known where groups have claimed to have committed particular terrorist acts in order to draw the attention of the mass media to themselves. Thus, even in the case of only one claimant, those having committed the act receive only part of the publicity involved, and possibly only a small part.

Effects of Diffusing Media Attention

The information strategy of refusing to attribute a terrorist attack to one particular group has systematic effects on the behaviour of terrorists. The benefits derived from having committed a terrorist act decrease for the group having undertaken it. The group does not reap the public attention it hoped to get. The political goals it wants to publicise are not propagated as much as desired. This reduction in publicity makes the terrorist act (to a certain degree) pointless, as modern terrorism essentially depends on publicity. Terrorists who are ready to take high risks – and even risk death – in order to publicise their political beliefs, feel deeply dissatisfied. The frustration is intensified by the feeling that other political groups, not so 'brave' as to have run the risk of undertaking terrorist acts, profit from free riding. They reap the benefits of increased publicity free of charge. This frustration is often intense, because terrorist groups tend to be in strong competition with each other, even when they have similar political beliefs. None of them is prepared to tolerate undertaking dangerous actions that another group receives the credit for. Most terrorist groups would prefer that no one is credited than that the publicity goes to another rival terrorist group. The authorities in charge of fighting terrorism may exploit this rivalry among terrorist groups by pointing out to the media that, among the likely perpetrators of a particular terrorist act, there may be terrorist groups known to be in competition with each other.

When the government's strategy reduces the rewards for terrorist acts, the terrorist groups concerned may react in three possible ways.

1. The terrorists may make an effort to claim responsibility for a terrorist act by providing appropriate 'proof'. This can, for instance, be done by providing photographs (for example showing a hostage with a newspaper of a particular date, as was done in the case of the kidnapping of Schleyer in Germany). The authorities, knowing well that such photographs are easy to fake, will have to point out that this is not adequate 'proof' and, in many instances, can produce similar 'proof' presented by other claimants. While the initial attempt to claim responsibility undoubtedly receives considerable public attention, this will also be true for the possible counter-evidence provided by the authorities. Terrorists may also try to establish proof by getting into direct contact with journalists. Such action involves considerable risk, because the terrorists have to venture out into the open and this renders them an easier target for normal police activity. The terrorists cannot, for example, discount the possibility of one of the journalists leaking information to the police of a planned meeting.

2. The terrorists switch to a more overt type of terrorist activity in

order to make sure that its originator is established beyond doubt. Such behaviour increases the risk of being caught by the police.

3. The terrorists desist from further terrorist activity, because it does not pay off, and switch to a non-violent way of pursuing and publicising their demands.

Each of these three reactions results in a decrease of terrorism, either because the terrorists choose to desist from further violent action or because the police are in a better position to detect and apprehend them.

The strategy of diffusing media attention also leads to a change in the behaviour of the government. Most importantly, as long as the originator of a terrorist act is not clearly established, the government does not have to yield to the demands being made. As long as it can argue that it does not know which of the conflicting demands should be fulfilled, it does not even have to reject any demands. In the case of kidnappings, this means that there is little risk that the terrorists respond by killing the hostages, as they would not gain anything by doing so; thus no ransom has to be paid. If political terrorists demand that some announcement be read on TV or published in newspapers, permission may even be granted, provided several announcements by different terrorist groups are arranged, thus strongly reducing the effect of any particular announcement.

The anti-terrorist policy proposed here has the great advantage of allowing the government to take the *initiative*. It can actively take steps to reduce the attention the terrorists receive from the media and the public. The terrorists become frustrated if they are not suitably rewarded for the risky terrorist acts, desist from further activities, or increasingly expose themselves to ordinary counter-terrorist methods by the police. The amount of terrorism will decrease; the dissatisfaction with existing political and social conditions will be expressed in different, less violent ways.

Possible Counter-arguments Against Diffusing Media Attention

The strategy of diffusing media attention by supplying more information than desired by the terrorists may be objected to on various grounds.

- The public expects, and has a right, to be accurately informed by the government about public affairs, and that includes terrorism. The strategy of leaving all possibilities open until the truth is established in court looks as if information was withheld, as no one particular terrorist group is presented as the perpetrator. In order to overcome this (mistaken) feeling, the government must make clear that there are, of necessity, always a number of different suspects and that, in a democratic society, it is solely the authority of the courts to establish who is guilty. The fact that there are several likely terrorist aggressors does not allow the focus to be on only one of them.

- The strategy based on refusing recognition is relevant for clandestine terrorist acts, such as kidnapping with an *unknown* hiding place, and bombings. This is an advantage rather than a disadvantage, because 'most expert knowledge to date deals with hostage situations in which the site of the hostage is known. Where the site is unknown, operational strategies and tactics are much less clear-cut and well-developed' (Crelinsten and Szabo, 1979: 81). The strategy is not as applicable for overt kidnapping, where the hostages are held in a publicly known place. The government can still argue that the hijackers, say of a plane or ship, are not fully identified, and that there are competing claims as to who they really are and what cause they really champion. However, the possibility of using such a strategy is more limited than in the case of clandestine terrorist activities. The strategy used is complementary to, and does not substitute for, ordinary police activities, which can be used to combat open terrorist actions, such as attacks by appropriately trained and armed forces.

- The strategy of diffusing media attention is also inapplicable if the terrorists only want to produce general chaos and uncertainty. In that case, terrorists derive no utility if their movement and their political goals are identified. At the same time, such terrorist acts have little effect, as the demands of the terrorists remain opaque. Normally, due to the 'rallying 'round the flag' effect, the government's position is strengthened. It receives more power to implement an anti-terrorist policy.

- The politicians in government and their chiefs of police tend to be reluctant to point to a number of different terrorist groups as aggressors. Such action gives the impression to the public that the authorities are incompetent. They do not appear capable of identifying which group is responsible for the terrorist act concerned. The politicians and public authorities in charge prefer to state that they are well informed and that they will soon be able to capture the terrorists, even if this is wishful thinking rather than reality.

- An anti-terrorist strategy of reducing the benefits to the terrorists of undertaking violent acts has the disadvantage that the resulting decline in terrorism is not directly attributed to the government and its agencies. All of them would much prefer to be directly credited. A competent government may, however, be able to attribute the success of the anti-terrorist policy to their actions, particularly by pointing out its *success*. In times of crisis, the various parties in a democracy tend to reach a consensus with respect to anti-terror policy. The government is insulated from party competition for some time. This was clearly the case after the attacks of September 11, 2001. President George W. Bush's popularity rose to unknown heights. The Democratic Party sided totally with the president's anti-terrorist policy for at least a year. The opposition feared that the slightest criticism would be interpreted as 'anti-American', or even national treason. This suggests that, even in a democracy with otherwise intensive political competition, the government would be able to pursue the strategy suggested here. It is, however, not necessary to rely only on the enlightened self-interest of the government. Laws prohibiting an unproven accusation of having committed a terrorist act may be introduced or strengthened, and it must also apply to the public authorities, including the police. As a result, the authorities would be more careful of attributing a terrorist act to a particular group. Rather, it would force them to indicate other possible actors. The laws should make it quite clear that only the courts have the right to establish who is guilty. Once the courts have decided, the group who actually committed the crime is identified – but the media have by then lost much of their interest. In a world characterised by many news items, and among them many atrocities, the amount of attention paid by the mass media and the public is normally short lived. In most cases, even major spectacular terrorist events capture the attention of the media and their consumers' attention for no more than seven to nine days.

Application to the Terrorist Attacks of September 11, 2001

The terrorist attacks on New York's twin towers and the Pentagon provide a case in which the anti-terrorist policy catapulted one particular group, *al Qaeda*, into the limelight of the media. This terrorist group and its goals were not generally known before, either in the United States or elsewhere. Few people beyond specialists on terrorism knew about the group – obviously it was not even well enough known to prevent the terrorists being given permission to enter the US and later having the possibility of hijacking planes.

All this changed dramatically on September 11. Even before the World Trade Center towers had collapsed, the government informed the media that the attacks were due to *al Qaeda*. All of a sudden, this terrorist group became more prominent than any terrorist group ever before in history. For the billions viewing the events on television and the week-long exclusive media attention on the attack, *al Qaeda* became a household name. Almost every adult in the world has heard of its leader, Osama Bin Laden. In a number of countries, he has become a hero. In the United States, the bookstores featured more books on Bin Laden than on any other living person, including President Bush. The subsequent war on Afghanistan was explicitly directed against Bin Laden.

This publicity effect in favour of a terrorist group is the result of an anti-terrorist policy seeking to prematurely identify the perpetrators. It propelled *al Qaeda* and Bin Laden into a position of prominence they could only have dreamed of. In this regard, the terrorists reached their goals, quite irrespective of whether they have to pay for their misdeeds later. This prominence was not due to the terrorist attack as such, but rather to the way the incident was handled by the American administration. Indeed, this is exactly what an official report by the Library of Congress, written in 1999, warned of: 'A U.S. counterterrorist policy, therefore, should avoid making leaders like Osama Bin Laden heroes or martyrs for Muslims' (Hudson, 1999: 65).

A different approach, along the lines suggested here, can well be imagined. The government could have pointed out that many terrorist groups *might* have had an interest in undertaking the attack. For the convenience of the media focused on 'personalities', several such names could have been mentioned, including, but not solely, Bin Laden. He would have been only one among many persons, and he would have remained one of many terrorists. This would not have pre-

vented the American government from engaging in a 'war on terrorism'. No lying is involved, because it is true that many different terrorist groups could have and would have liked to have undertaken the
attack. The major terrorist events, costing the lives of hundreds of
persons in Bali (in 2002) and Moscow (in 2002), illustrate that *al
Qaeda* and Bin Laden (who might have been dead by then) are certainly not the only dangerous terrorists.

Comparison to Conventional Anti-terrorist Policies

There are various major differences between the strategy of diffusing
media attention and conventional anti-terrorist policy.

- The strategy is active and the government forces the terrorists
  to react. Most conventional anti-terrorist policies are, in contrast, reactive. The terrorists dictate the procedure and the
  terms under which the interaction takes place.
- The strategy refuses to give terrorists the rewards that go with
  public attention. The current policy tends to publicise and
  'officially' acknowledge the importance of the terrorist group
  and thereby its cause.
- The strategy lowers the rewards for undertaking terrorist
  actions. Terrorists' incentives to engage in future violent acts
  are reduced. The current government anti-terrorist policy
  invites future terrorism in so far as it has met terrorist demands
  in the past.
- The strategy does not violate the freedom of the press and of
  the other media. Current anti-terrorist policy tends to suppress
  or reduce free reporting.
- The strategy does not infringe on human rights and civil liberties. The current anti-terrorist policy, with its emphasis on the
  heavy use of police power and on modern methods of investigation and surveillance, is bound to reduce citizens' rights.

The discussion suggests that fighting terrorism by diffusing media
attention may be a useful addition to existing policies. It is not an
alternative to existing policy in the sense that it would render police
action unnecessary. However, it constitutes a clear alternative with
respect to how information is to be handled. The strategy of diffusing the attention of the media may be openly discussed; its effect does

not depend on the fact that the terrorists know about it. Rather, one of its remarkable features is that it is largely immune to counter-strategies.

SUGGESTED FURTHER READING

Most books on terrorism deal with the role of the media. The following analyses are particularly useful:

Wilkinson, Paul (2000). *Terrorism Versus Democracy: The Liberal State Response.* London: Frank Cass, Chapter 5.
Hoffman, Bruce (1998). *Inside Terrorism.* New York: Columbia University Press, Chapter 9.
Crelinsten, Ronald D. (1990). 'Terrorism and the Media: Problems, Solutions and Counterproblems'. In Charters, David A. (ed.) (1990). *Democratic Response to International Terrorism.* Ardsley-on-Hudson, New York: Transatlantic Publishers, pp. 267–307.

The role of the media and the provision of information in dealing with current terrorism are also discussed in:

Gentzkow, Matthew and Jesse M. Shapiro (2004). 'Media, Education, and Anti-Americanism in the Muslim World'. *Journal of Economic Perspectives*, forthcoming.

The systematic overestimation of the dangers of terrorism is also discussed in:

Viscusi, W. Kip and Richard J. Zeckhauser (2003). 'Sacrificing Civil Liberties to Reduce Terrorism Risks'. *Journal of Risk and Uncertainty* **26**(2–3): 99–120.
Congleton, Roger D. (2002). 'Terrorism, Interest-group Politics, and Public Policy: Curtailing Criminal Modes of Political Speech'. *Independent Review* **7**(1): 47–67.

Various kinds of intervention in the media are documented in:

Alexander, Yonah and Richard Latter (eds) (1990). *Terrorism and the Media.* Washington, DC: Brassey's.

The policy of diffusing media attention, by supplying more information than desired by the terrorists, was first proposed in:

Frey, Bruno S. (1988). 'Fighting Political Terrorism by Refusing Recognition'. *Journal of Public Policy* **7**: 179–88. Reprinted in Bruno S.

Frey, Bruno S. (1999). *Economics as a Science of Human Behaviour*, 2nd revised and extended edn. Boston and Dordrecht: Kluwer, pp. 99–108.

Major terrorist events, in which no group claimed responsibility, are reported in:

Lesser, Ian O., Bruce Hoffman, John Arquilla, David F. Ronfeldt, Michele Zanini and Brian Michael Jensen (1999). *Countering the New Terrorism*. Santa Monica, CA: Rand Corporation.

PART IV

What Can Be Done?

There are many different strategies available for anti-terrorist policy. Chapter 8 points out that there is no need to restrict policies on deterrence; the positive approaches presented are suitable, and in many respects superior, alternatives.

The four policies discussed here – deterrence and the positive policies of polycentricity, the provision of positive incentives for renouncing terrorism and dispersing media attention – are compared using six criteria: the time required, effectiveness, costs, efficiency, legal and moral considerations. In a society with many different views and interests, it is impossible to determine which policy is best. Rather, rules need to be found which enable decisions on anti-terrorist policies to be taken. However, combining the four policies may not be easy, because they may clash with each other. In particular, a coercive policy tends to preclude the use of the positive approaches to anti-terrorist policies.

The concluding Chapter 9 notes that terrorism cannot be wiped out entirely, because there is a continuous innovative struggle between governments and terrorists.

A crucial question is why deterrence policy is so often undertaken, though it is far from successful. The reason is to be found in the fact that government politicians derive additional private benefits from using force. The same holds for the military, the police and the secret service. In contrast, the proponents of positive anti-terrorist policies are weak, at least in the short run. The outcome of the political struggle can be influenced by constitutional design. Most importantly, giving citizens more extensive participation rights makes governments more aware of the sharply increasing long-term costs of coercive policy, inducing them to consider alternatives more seriously and earlier on. Moreover, the constitution must prohibit the armed forces from interfering in politics.

A final plea is made for engaging in anti-terrorist policies based on a positive approach, producing interactions benefiting all sides long term.

8.   Comparing Anti-terrorist Policies

MANY OPTIONS

This book is devoted to suggesting *positive* options for dealing with terrorism. Such options have been neglected in the theoretical discourse on terrorism, as well as in the practical policies applied against terrorism. In contrast, the *negative* options of threatening and punishing terrorists have been at the centre of academic discussion, and even more at the centre of anti-terrorist policy. It often seems as if deterrence policy is a hard-wired knee-jerk reaction to terrorism, while other, more novel approaches receive only cursory attention. The positive approach proposed here is based on modern economics; it first seeks to understand why and how terrorists act. It looks at terrorists' preferences and constraints. Based on this incentive, structured anti-terrorist policies are deduced, promising to be both effective and advisable.

In view of the extensive scholarly work on terrorism, there is no need to repeat many aspects of the phenomena that appear. Thus, for example, technological aspects of terrorism, ranging from weapons of mass destruction, to cyber and internet terrorism, were only considered in so far as they directly relate to the policies discussed. The same applies to psychological operations on the one hand, and military operations (including executing adversaries) on the other hand. The fact that these aspects are not discussed in this book does not mean that they are unimportant, but rather that they have been ably dealt with elsewhere.

A particularly important aspect of terrorism relates to the *international coordination* of the fight against terrorism. Since the American government has identified *al Qaeda* as the perpetrator of the attacks on New York and Washington, as well as the support of the Taliban government of Afghanistan for it, the importance of home bases and safe havens for terrorists is well known. But this also applies to many

other terrorist organisations. The German *Rote Armee Fraktion* was
supported by the German Democratic Republic, and a considerable
number of its members found refuge there when the RAF collapsed.
In so far as terrorists act internationally – and this is the rule today –
an effective anti-terrorist policy must also cross national boundaries.
In the wake of September 11, 2001, the American government made
huge efforts to build a global coalition against terrorism. Many countries in the world quickly joined. While some of their political representatives may have yielded to the pressure imposed by today's
imperial power, most grasped the need for an international response
to terrorism.

There is no need to discuss the beneficial aspects of coordinating
the fight against terrorists at international level. But it should be
pointed out that such a policy may have an important negative consequence. The coalition necessarily includes some members with a
bad record where civil rights are concerned. Opposing such governments, perhaps even by resorting to terrorist actions, may be considered acceptable from the point of view of democratic countries. But
by virtue of being a member of the coalition against terrorism, such
governments have a free hand. They may even feel encouraged, and
are materially supported, to suppress such opposition by all means.
The term 'terrorist' then tends to be used for all groups not in agreement with the government. An example is the way the Russian
government deals with the opposition in Chechnya. The possibly
legitimate demand for self-rule is crushed by violent means in the
name of fighting international terrorism. The purpose of the fight
against terrorism is that democratic and peaceful means are used to
settle contending views. But violent behaviour against other political
views and goals in the name of anti-terrorist policy undermines the
whole purpose. The international coalition could be accused of not
acting any better than the terrorists themselves.

CRITERIA FOR ANTI-TERRORIST POLICIES

In the following, the anti-terrorist policies discussed will be evaluated
according to six different criteria: the time required, effectiveness,
cost, efficiency, legal and moral acceptability. (An important further
criterion, the incentives of governments to apply a particular policy,
will be discussed in the final chapter.) No complete classification of

the policies with respect to the six criteria is intended. Rather, only the major aspects are considered as to how the three anti-terrorist policies proposed here – polycentricity, positive incentives to renounce terrorism and dispersing media attention – and the conventional deterrence policy fare, when looked at from various points of view.

Time Required

A major advantage of a punitive approach is that it can quickly be put into effect. Most countries affected by terrorist acts have sufficiently large police and military forces to strike back within a short time – though it is not always clear whether actual terrorists or innocent persons are hit. Results in terms of the number of persons killed, and installations destroyed, are immediately visible. The reaction of the Israeli government to Palestinian terrorists and suicide bombers is a good example. Almost overnight, the villages and camps from which the terrorists are presumed to originate, as well as the homes of their presumed relatives, are demolished.

Most positive approaches, in contrast, take considerable time to be put into action and to show results. In the case of the polycentric policy, the time frame is large. It takes years to arrange for economic, political and social decision-making to be shared by many persons, and to be widely distributed over space. It also cannot be expected that offering incentives to potential and actual terrorists to give up violent action will show any quick results. To overcome mutual mistrust takes considerable time and does not proceed at a steady rate.

Effectiveness

An anti-terrorist policy able to significantly reduce terrorist violence can be called effective. Previous chapters have argued and proposed evidence that all three of the positive anti-terrorist policies are effective in this sense. The more polycentric a country is, the less vulnerable it is. The potential terrorists find it difficult, if not impossible, to find a worthwhile target with which they can terrorise the chosen enemy. Indeed, decentralisation has proved to be so effective that terrorists have copied it. *Al Qaeda*, for example, has the character of a virtual organisation. Its individual parts work independently to a large extent, and are ignorant (and therefore cannot reveal any information if captured) as to who the other parts are and what they do.

Such decentralisation on the part of terrorists makes it much more difficult for the police and army to act effectively against them. A decentralised method of financing the activities typical for modern terrorist organisations makes it nearly impossible to intercept the flow of resources used for terrorist purposes.

Offering positive incentives to terrorists to desist from their activities opens up new opportunities for them. It also undermines the coherence of the terrorist groups. Refusing to attribute a violent act to a particular terrorist group robs them of one of the crucial prizes of terrorism, unique media attention.

Reliance on deterrence policy has been tried very often but has, in many cases, yielded disappointing results. The use of punishment and retribution is unlikely to solve the problems underlying terrorist activities. Deterrence policy may even lead to counterproductive results. Violent action against actual or presumed terrorists tends to induce new persons to join, or at least support, terrorist groups. Already established terrorists see no valuable alternatives for themselves; they are locked in. Both well-established and new terrorists often seek revenge for the casualties suffered by their family, relatives and friends. Another reason for a possible counterproductive effect lies in increased political centralisation combined with deterrence policy. A policy based on negative sanctions *seems* to yield impressive results, as terrorists and their supporters (but also innocent people) are indeed killed and incarcerated. But the consequences *induced* in most cases do not lead to a reduction of terrorism. The very high punishments cited in the US anti-terrorist laws, instituted by President Reagan in 1984 (Public Law 98–473 and 98–553), is an example. Individuals taking US hostages, inside or outside the United States, face life imprisonment. The penalties for placing bombs aboard a plane or destroying an aircraft were also drastically increased. These laws proved, however, to have 'no statistical effect whatsoever against US-directed terrorist acts' (Enders, Sandler and Cauley, 1990a,1990b).

Cost

Anti-terrorist policies require the use of all kinds of resources. They may be material or immaterial, such as the attention and effort required by the government politicians to devise and implement specific programmes.

Deterrence policy requires substantial material resources. Potential and actual terrorists must be convinced that undertaking violent acts will carry a heavy penalty. The probability of being caught, and the punishment imposed, must be so high that terrorists find it preferable to desist or to undertake violent acts elsewhere. In the latter case, terrorism is exported rather than curbed. A threat never put into practice is not credible. A deterrence policy therefore involves the use of police and military forces to actually punish terrorists. The resources needed for these purposes are no longer available for other, more peaceful uses. These opportunity costs are often high. This holds particularly for poor countries, where a substantial part of GNP, and a high percentage of young men conscripted into the military service, are used for that purpose.

Different groups face quite different opportunity costs for engaging in deterrence policy. Politicians in government must consider the budgetary costs involved when fighting the terrorists. To finance deterrence policy, they must resort to unpopular tax increases, raise the public debt (with future burdens in the form of interest payments), or print additional money (thereby raising future inflation). The situation is quite different for the members of the police and military forces, especially for its officers and commanders. Their importance in society, and vis-à-vis the government, increases when they are given the task of fighting terrorists. They not only receive more material and human resources, but also directly gain by pay increases. In an 'all out war' against terrorism, they receive more competencies, often beyond the rule of law. Not surprisingly, the officers and commanders of the police and the military forces normally welcome a strong deterrence policy. Only when they realise over the course of time that they are unable to win against the terrorists do they tend to become more careful. They may sometimes even change sides if they expect that the (former) terrorists will become their new bosses.

Positive policies also carry costs. This is most obviously seen when rewarding actual and potential terrorists for renouncing violent acts. Such rewards are only effective if they are of sufficient magnitude. A policy of compensation involves substantial budgetary costs, whose costs are attributed to the government. But the terrorists may also be compensated for desisting from violent acts by giving them non-material rewards. In many cases, a successful policy has been to let them participate in political decision-making, offering them seats in parliament or even in government. The politicians in government incur costs because they then have to share power with the former terrorists.

The other two positive policies have comparatively low costs. Polycentricity involves a reduction in power of the former decision-makers in the centre. But it is likely to revitalise the economy and society by furthering competition and enabling more innovative enterprises. As the economic theory of federalism, and more generally market theory, has long argued, political and economic decentralisation further the growth of income and reduce unemployment. Even if decentralisation is undertaken as part of anti-terrorist policy, the beneficial effects can still be reaped. Dispersing media attention, by offering more information in case of a terrorist act, carries low costs. The police and secret service can easily name a number of possible perpetrators.

Efficiency

Welfare maximising and rational political decision-makers would consider both the effectiveness and the cost of various anti-terrorist policies. They favour policies with high effectiveness and low cost and reject those with low effectiveness and high cost. None of the four policies considered here uniquely qualifies for one of these categories. It follows that each of the policies may be efficient under certain conditions. For instance, when police and military forces already exist, and terrorists are pursuing a cause without much support from the people, and the danger of further terrorist acts is imminent, a sanctioning policy may be best. If, on the other hand, terrorists exploit existing grievous social conditions, and have the active or passive support of a sizeable part of the people, a positive policy is far more effective.

In reality, of course, governments are neither welfare maximising nor fully rational. They therefore only partially consider effectiveness and the overall economic and social cost of anti-terrorist policies. Rather, they evaluate effectiveness and costs with regard to how they affect their own utility, in particular their re-election chances. As Public Choice theory has established, this leads to serious deviations from effectiveness. Moreover, not all costs to the members of society as a whole also represent costs for the government. This is, for instance, not the case when government anti-terror expenditures lead to revenue for firms and other actors supporting the government undertaking these expenditures.

Legal Aspects

Anti-terrorist policies may violate national laws and constitutional provisions, as well as internationally agreed human rights and laws on war. The danger of such an eventuality is endemic in the case of deterrence policy. Often, it is undertaken without regard to such legal constraints. It is argued that the danger of terrorism is so great that these rules must be violated for the sake of protecting the state. It is obvious, however, that legal rules are often broken, because it is in the personal interests of government politicians, as well as the police and the military.

The situation is quite different for an anti-terrorist policy based on strengthening polycentricity. Such a policy is compatible with both national and international law. To disperse media attention is not illegal. Indeed, the government and the police break the law by attributing a violent attack to a particular terrorist group. In a liberal society, following the rule of law, as long as the *courts* have not established responsibility, even suspected perpetrators must be given the benefit of the doubt. To point out that a number of different groups *may* be responsible for a terrorist act therefore fully corresponds to desirable policy in a liberal society.

Offering compensation to terrorists for giving up future violent action, instead of punishing them for their past deeds, may appear to be illegal. But, in most countries, the heads of the state, or the courts, have the power to absolve persons for having broken the law. Not punishing terrorists is legal and legitimate, if such action reduces further harm and if it can safely be expected that they will be reintegrated back into society.

Moral Considerations

What is taken to be 'moral' differs from one person to another. Some persons believe it to be moral to punish terrorists and therefore advocate a strict sanctioning policy. Others believe it to be moral to forgive past 'sins', even if they had deadly consequences. They therefore support policies helping to reintegrate terrorists back into normal life by offering rewards. Others believe that it is the duty of government and police to indicate which terrorist group has most probably committed a particular violent act. They therefore reject a policy of naming various groups as possible perpetrators. Others are convinced that it is deeply immoral to give terrorists so much media attention, and therefore prefer a policy of not pinpointing a particular group.

This discussion suggests that it is not possible to decide on the basis of moral considerations which anti-terrorist policy is morally defensible; it all depends on a person's underlying fundamental ideology. This does not mean that morals should play no role when deciding how to tackle terrorism. But each person has to decide for him- or herself; there is no overriding 'social moral' pointing in the right direction.

THE PROBLEM OF EVALUATION

None of the four anti-terrorist policies is 'the best' in the sense that one of them should dominate the other three with respect to all six criteria. This applies also to deterrence policy, though it is all too often assumed to be the only possible, or at least rational, response to terrorism. Nor is it possible to find a ranking of the four policies acceptable to all persons concerned. It has been pointed out, for instance, that the use of negative sanctions may entail higher costs to government politicians than to the leaders of the military and police forces. The discussion reveals that engaging more in one anti-terrorist policy and less in another makes some people better off, and other people worse off.

This result is not surprising: in society, persons have many different views with respect to what collective actions, including anti-terrorist policies, are desirable. Social Choice Theory has established that it is not generally possible to derive a consistent social 'welfare function' and hence 'social choice' from individuals' heterogeneous preferences in a democracy. A dictator may, of course, take a unilateral decision, but this will not reflect the preferences of the people he or she claims to represent. Voting by majority, or by any other voting mechanism, also does not solve the basic preference aggregation problem. It cannot be excluded that inconsistent choices arise.

The preference aggregation problem also prohibits simply assigning weights to each criterion. This is often done by assigning higher numbers to 'more important', and lower numbers to 'less important' criteria, and then scaling the degree to which each policy fulfils a particular criterion. The mechanistic addition of these numbers only seemingly identifies a socially desirable policy. The 'winning' policy has no meaning in a democracy and, in actual fact, once determined, tends to be strongly opposed by those persons whose preferences are disregarded.

Constitutional Political Economy provides a solution to the problem of choosing between various anti-terrorist policies in a democracy. It takes a step back. Instead of trying to evaluate how valuable the policies are on the aggregate level, it chooses the rules under which this decision takes place. The basic insight is that it is easier to decide about the rules governing a decision than to determine the outcome. To prevent individuals choosing the decision rule according to the most favourable outcome for themselves, people are placed behind a 'veil of ignorance' with respect to the decisions to be taken in the future. Nobody knows whether they will be among the citizens victimised by the terrorists, will fight on the side of the terrorists, will not be directly involved, or will be a member of the military or police. Behind this veil of ignorance, individuals are able to discuss the advantages and disadvantages of the rules governing various anti-terrorist policies, without knowing their own preferences. This state can be approximated by various means, for instance by having old people, with no direct stake in the future, decide on the decision rules to be applied or, preferably, determine a decision procedure which will come into force only in the future.

In stable democracies, these decision rules have been determined in a generally accepted constitution. It specifies the overall conditions to be followed in the event of a terrorist threat. The *political process* to be followed is determined. This indirectly also determines how trade-offs are to be dealt with. The constitution may possibly give special powers to the existing government to enable a swift response in times of imminent danger. But, in a democracy, it will also establish safeguards that the government does not violate important human rights. It also ensures that the government relinquishes the extra power once the terrorist danger has been reduced. Most importantly, it involves the citizens in a discussion process, in which the advantages and disadvantages of the various anti-terrorist policies can be openly discussed.

The criteria discussed serve a crucial purpose in such a democratic discussion process. They serve as 'inputs' into the political decision-making process by informing the citizens about the likely properties and consequences of the various anti-terrorist policies. The citizens need to be made aware that there are viable alternatives to the knee-jerk reaction of hitting back at terrorists by using negative sanctions. An evaluation of the anti-terrorist policies in terms of the various criteria helps citizens to participate in an informed, and more rational way in the democratic discussion process.

COMBINING ANTI-TERRORIST STRATEGIES

So far, the four strategies dealing with terrorism have been considered independently. It has, in particular, been argued that the positive policies have several important advantages over a deterrence policy based on negative sanctions. But it stands to reason that a good overall policy combines all of these, and uses each one where its advantages outweigh its disadvantages.

Such a combination of various strategies is indeed possible for those policies largely independent of each other. Thus, for example, the policy of providing positive incentives to terrorists to desist from their actions is compatible with a policy of political, economic and social decentralisation. In general, the chances of being able to combine the policies relying on a positive approach are good, because they start with the same basic premise.

In contrast, deterrence policy is difficult to combine with the positive approaches of the other three anti-terrorist policies. The use of force to a considerable extent tends to undermine positively oriented anti-terrorist policies. An effort to hit the (presumed) perpetrators hard and fast is often incompatible with arguing that several different terrorist groups may be responsible for a particular terrorist incident. Most importantly, seeking to punish terrorists by capturing, incarcerating or killing them is inconsistent with offering them positive incentives to desist from further violence and reintegrating them back into society.

However, the policies using force, and those relying on positive incentives can, to some extent, be employed consecutively. Terrorists may be offered rewards for not committing any future violence. If they do not accept the offer, or do not conform sufficiently, force cannot only be threatened, but used. But such an approach runs the risk that the terrorists mainly perceive it as coercive, and therefore are not prepared to enter into positive interaction. The willingness to engage in a mutually beneficial relationship tends to be crowded out by the threatened use of force. The opposite time sequence is more promising. A punishing reaction after terrorists have committed an act of violence is followed by a well-orchestrated and clear offer of rewards to terrorists if they desist from such actions in the future. The door is opened to possible future interaction, based on positive attitudes. But the government's coercive response may possibly harden the position of the terrorists so much that they are unwilling, or unable, to engage in more positive interactions later on. The consecutive use of coercive and positive policies thus does not always lead to the desired outcome of effectively reducing terrorism. The appeal of using many different approaches to overcome terrorism is well-taken but not simple to apply effectively.

SUGGESTED FURTHER READING

Technological aspects of terrorism, in particular the use of biological, chemical and nuclear weapons, as well as cyber-terrorism, are well explained, for instance, in:

Hoffman, Bruce (1998). *Inside Terrorism*. New York: Columbia University Press.
Kushner, Harvey W. (ed.) (1998). *The Future of Terrorism: Violence in the New Millennium*. London: Sage Publications.
Lesser, Ian O., Bruce Hoffman, John Arquilla, David F. Ronfeldt, Michele Zanini and Brian Michael Jensen (1999). *Countering the New Terrorism*. Santa Monica, CA: Rand Corporation.

Psychological warfare against terrorists is treated in:

Schmid, Alex P. and Ronald D. Crelinsten (eds) (1993). *Western Responses to Terrorism*. London: Frank Cass.

The use of force, by executing terrorist leaders and their supporters, is dealt with by:

Byman, Daniel L. and Matthew C. Waxman (2002). *The Dynamics of Coercion. American Foreign Policy and the Limits of Military Power*. Cambridge: Cambridge University Press.

An extensive discussion of international cooperation and conventions to overcome terrorism can be found in:

Wilkinson, Paul (2000). *Terrorism Versus Democracy: The Liberal State Response*. London: Frank Cass.

Sandler, Todd (2003). 'Collective Action and Transnational Terrorism'. *World Economy* 26: 779–802.

The decentralisation strategy of various terrorist organisations is identified in:

Lesser, Ian O., Bruce Hoffman, John Arquilla, David F. Ronfeldt, Michele Zanini and Brian Michael Jensen (1999). *Countering the New Terrorism.* Santa Monica, CA: Rand Corporation.
Arquilla, John and David Ronfeldt (2001). *Networks and Netwars: The Future of Terror, Crime, and Militancy.* Santa Monica, CA: Rand Corporation.

The general impossibility of aggregating individual preferences to a social welfare or social decision function has been proved by:

Arrow, Kenneth J. (1951). *Social Choice and Individual Values.* New York: John Wiley & Sons.
Sen, Amartya K. (1970). *Collective Choice and Social Welfare.* Republished, Amsterdam: North Holland (1979), San Francisco: Holden-Day.

Constitutional economics has been shaped by:

Buchanan, James M. and Gordon Tullock (1962). *The Calculus of Consent. Logical Foundations of Constitutional Democracy.* Ann Arbor, MI: University of Michigan Press.
Buchanan, James M. (1991). *Constitutional Economics.* Oxford: Basil Blackwell.

Monographs on economic policy following these principles are:

Cooter, Robert D. (2000). *The Strategic Constitution.* Princeton, NJ: Princeton University Press.
Mueller, Dennis C. (1996). *Constitutional Democracy.* New York: Oxford University Press.
Frey, Bruno S. (1983). *Democratic Economic Policy.* Oxford: Blackwell.

An application of constitutional principles to dealing with terrorism has been put forward by:

Mueller, Dennis C. (2003a). 'Rights and Citizenship in a World of Global Terrorism'. Mimeo, Department of Economics, University of Vienna.

The concept of the veil of ignorance is due to:

Rawls, John (1971). *A Theory of Justice.* Cambridge, MA: Harvard University Press.

The role of discussion among citizens for reaching social decisions has been emphasised by:

Habermas, Jürgen (1992). *Faktizität und Geltung: Beiträge zur Diskurstheorie des Rechts und des demokratischen Rechtsstaates*. Frankfurt: Suhrkamp.

9. Conclusions

A CONTINUOUS STRUGGLE

It is impossible to imagine a world without terrorism. There will always be groups and individuals wanting to further their cause by violent means. 'Dealing with terrorism' does not mean its total elimination, but rather reducing the number and severity of terrorist acts, and mitigating its effects. The objective must be to contain and manage terrorism.

No policy can eradicate terrorism. This holds even when the government, in conjunction with the military, the police and the secret services, uses the most extreme coercive measures. Terrorists learn and quickly adjust to new policies and circumstances. They are innovative and able to identify and exploit new vulnerabilities. Due to the small size of their operational units, they are not restricted by bureaucratic rules and regulations. This enables them often to adjust more quickly than the anti-terrorist side, frustrating or defeating the security measures put in place. As a result, many terrorist groups are able to inflict a huge amount of damage with little cost to their own side. The attacks of September 11, 2001 on the World Trade towers and Pentagon are a case in point. The direct and indirect human and economic costs were large in absolute terms, while the costs to the terrorists were minimal. They were able to use an innovation (kidnapping large civilian aircraft and using them as rockets directed against seemingly stable skyscrapers) with devastating effect. The fact that the techniques were rather primitive (it was relatively simple to overwhelm the crew and to steer the planes into the towers) does not mean that they were not effective. Of course, anti-terror policy has now made *this* particular violent act more difficult and unlikely. But if the terrorists were able to undertake that innovation on one occasion, it is rational to expect that they will be able to do so again in the future. Even rather unsophisticated and inexpensive weapons may be used to great effect. In 1981, Puerto Rican terrorists invaded the Muniz Air National Guard Base in Puerto Rico. By using simple explosive devices, they destroyed and damaged 11 fighter aircraft, inflicting a financial loss of more than 45 million dollars (Lesser et al., 1999). The bomb planted in 1993 in the basement of one of the towers of the World Trade Center cost only 400 dollars. It was sheer luck that the tower did not topple, which would have resulted in 550 million dollars in damages (Hoffman, 1998). But there is not only a huge cost asymmetry. Terrorists can choose to target a particularly vulnerable point where they have high expectations of success. Terrorism is, in this sense, cost-effective. Moreover, the terrorists can make many attempts at hitting the adversary, while the target country must try to prevent *any* major attack. Indeed, terrorists intended using commercial aircraft as bombs on a number of occasions before September 11, 2001. In 1986, a Pan American Boeing 747 was hijacked at Karachi airport with the idea of crashing it into a city in Israel. The plan could not be put into practice because the plane was stormed before take-off. The terrorists' intentions were revealed during the trial in 1988 (Mickolus et al., 1989).

The highly decentralised structure of terrorists' organisations is another example of a successful innovation. *Al Qaeda* is closer to a modern 'virtual organisation' than most international firms are. This extreme form of decentralisation makes it difficult to locate, fight and annihilate them.

Historical experience reveals that no side has a definite advantage in this innovative struggle. This is what makes terrorism so dangerous. Significant advances in counter-terrorist approaches have always been matched by new terrorist techniques.

WHAT ARE THE INCENTIVES FOR POLICY-MAKERS?

Coercive deterrence has been identified in this book as being far from effective. It has high human, material, legal and moral costs, and may even lead to counterproductive results. On the other hand, positive anti-terrorist policies promise more favourable results with fewer costs.

The crucial questions then are: Why is coercive deterrence so often undertaken? Why are the more beneficial policies so rarely used? In order to answer these questions, it is necessary to look at the incentive structure of the actors involved. This refers most importantly to the government, but also to the law enforcing agencies, including the military forces, as well as groups opposing deterrence policy.

Government

It has often been argued that, in democracies, governments are unable
to pursue a long-term policy because of the restricted election term
of (mostly) four years. Following this argument, democratic governments are prone to undertake coercive deterrence strategies against
terrorists. They are best able to achieve quick 'successes' (even if they
are more apparent than real, and reduce long-term prospects of
reducing terrorist activities). The implication is that only authoritarian, or even dictatorial, governments are able to undertake long-term
anti-terrorist policies. While the introduction of such regimes in order
to fight terrorism is rarely openly proposed, it is nevertheless claimed
that democratic governments must receive extraordinary powers. For
example, while it is a fundamental principle of democracies to abso-
lutely prohibit the use of torture, it is argued that it may be used
against actual or presumed terrorists.

This view is, however, mistaken. Democratic governments have a
time frame extending beyond the four-year election period. They
often have a good chance of being re-elected, which extends their
term in power. Moreover, the party in government takes into account
the effects the policies pursued will have on their reputation. This
again extends the time frame. Authoritarian and dictatorial governments do not necessarily have a longer time frame. Indeed, it tends to
be lower, because they can be subject to a coup at any time. As a consequence, they have to go to great lengths to constantly secure their
power, which induces them to undertake short-run anti-terrorist policies.

While there is little systematic difference between democratic and
authoritarian regimes with respect to time frames, there are various
factors making governments favour a coercive anti-terrorist policy.

- The use of force sometimes appears to be the only conceivable
  reaction to a violent terrorist act. This applies, in particular,
  when the act is ongoing, such as when terrorists kidnap
  persons. In such situations, the people demand leadership and
  determined political action, which is best exhibited by using the
  police and military forces. People rally around their flag and
  support governments willing to defend it. Politicians of all per-
  suasions easily succumb to the temptation of showing much-
  applauded 'macho' behaviour. Other policies are easily seen as

showing weakness. Authoritarian and dictatorial governments, based to some extent on domestic coercion, cannot tolerate a challenge to their power by terrorists without responding aggressively.

- Governments may fear that not using force against terrorists undermines the basis of democracy. In contrast, compromise is identified with capitulation. Often, it is identified with the 'Munich' agreement, in which the British Prime Minister, Neville Chamberlain, yielded to the demands of Hitler, only to find out that this behaviour invited Hitler to make further territorial demands.

- An aggressive anti-terrorist policy, engaging the police and the military, allows governments to draw attention away from domestic problems, especially from unsatisfactory economic conditions. The Falklands/Malvinas War decisively helped the Conservative Party under Margaret Thatcher to win the UK general election in 1982. Responding forcefully and engaging in violent actions sometimes appears to be the only chance for governments to survive. This does not only apply to dictators, but to some extent also to politicians in democratic countries. Democratic politicians are well versed in exploiting the chances offered by terrorist attacks. President Bush secured the Republican Party a resounding victory in the mid-term congressional elections in November 2002, due to his 'crusade' and later 'war against terrorism'.

- Using force to fight terrorism provides the government with new competencies and resources. This increases its domestic and international power.

Other Groups Supporting Deterrence Policy

The military, the police and the secret services derive substantial and immediate benefits from a coercive policy. They get even more resources than the government, including pay increases and more competencies. This considerably enhances their position in society. They are therefore strong supporters of the use of force to combat terrorists. In addition to receiving these economic and social benefits, they support the use of force because they have been trained and indoctrinated in this direction. They are often not even aware that alternative anti-terrorist strategies exist. Many of the persons voluntarily serving in these forces, the professional soldiers, constitute a particular section of the population, those who like using coercive means. As a consequence, they tend to have an ingrained ideology focused on deterrence.

Proponents of Positive Approaches

Only politically weak groups favour the positive approaches outlined, in particular immediately after a terrorist attack has occurred. Among them are civil rights groups concerned with the violation of human rights, some churches and individual scholars.

This situation only changes when the costs of a coercive policy begin to be felt by the people. The dissatisfaction with the anti-terrorist policy employed may at first be barely visible and restricted to only a few groups, in particular students who run the risk of being drafted for military service. However, well-organised groups may also take part in protests, for instance the trade unions. It is also likely, of course, that the military will be demoralised by a 'war' they consider impossible to win. They may also resent the 'dirty' measures involved in a military fight against terrorists, among them the use of torture and the pre-emptive killing of possibly innocent persons. They rightly perceive such actions to be inconsistent with their sense of military honour.

Institutional Design

Individuals adjust their behaviour in systematic ways to changes in the constraints imposed. The preference for coercive deterrence policy can be mitigated or overcome by adequately setting the institutional conditions within which individuals act. In order to give the positive anti-terrorist deterrence policy more leeway, deterrence policy needs to be made less attractive. This can be achieved by making the ineffectiveness and the long-term costs of this policy more visible. As a result, coercion is used less in the short term, and positive anti-terrorist policies stand a better chance.

The government's motivation can be affected by strengthening its dependence on voters' preferences. The government has a stronger preference for a coercive policy than the people, because the politicians in power derive specific, *private* benefits from employing forceful means. These benefits are not enjoyed by the population as a whole. Governments therefore have too strong an incentive to undertake a coercive anti-terrorist policy. When politicians are more strongly bound to voters' preferences, the incentives to engage in a deterrence policy are reduced. Moreover, governments need to reckon with the longer term consequences of their own behaviour, which favours an earlier switch to positive anti-terrorist policies. Finally, the more the government's fate depends on the will of the voters, the less is it dominated by the demands of the military, police and secret services, which again derive special, *private* benefits. The *negative external effects* produced by the government and its agencies, and imposed on the people by deterrence policy, can be mitigated by strengthening the political influence of citizens. They can be given the right to directly influence issues via referenda and initiatives; that is, by institutions of (semi-) direct democracy.

In many countries, especially those of the Third World, the military often strongly influence politics. As a result, the use of force against terrorists prevails. The constitution should expressly forbid such non-democratic intervention. Political decision-making is to be left to the citizens and the civilian politicians as their representatives.

Anti-terrorist policies, relying on a positive approach, can be given a better chance by constitutionally guaranteeing the freedom of the media. TV, radio stations and newspapers, in competition with each other, enable dissenting views to be freely reported and allow them to be better heard. The ensuing public discussion makes it possible to better appreciate the disadvantages of coercive policies, and to grasp the advantages of positive policies.

The position taken here differs greatly from what is often demanded, and what often happens in reality. The fight against terrorism tends to involve a move towards less democratic means of governance. It is often claimed that no success is possible unless human rights are curtailed, including torturing and killing persons presumed to be terrorists. In contrast, *more democracy* is required here: it works to reduce the infatuation with coercion, and it improves the scope for more positive approaches of dealing with terrorism.

A PLEA FOR A POSITIVE APPROACH

Politics, as well as much of scholarly analysis, have been committed to fighting terrorism by deterrence. An alternative view has been presented here.

Decentralising economic, political and social centres of decision-making markedly reduces the incentives for potential terrorists to attack. Polycentricity enables the various parts of society to compensate quickly for any damage done. Terrorists are aware that decentralisation makes a country to some extent invulnerable. They realise that a terrorist attack will not have much effect on the target. The amount of costs imposed by a terrorist attack much depends on the reaction of the victims. If the government of the country attacked responds by itself interrupting economic activities (for example by closing down commercial air traffic and the stock exchange), and by embarking on a deterrence policy, the costs on the victimised country will be much larger. This, in turn, offers incentives to potential terrorists to attack. In contrast, governments confident in the self-stabilising nature of a polycentric society, will intervene less in the economy, polity and society, and will therefore keep the expected costs of a possible terrorist attack low. This, in turn, reduces the incentives for terrorists to attack.

The incentives of terrorists to attack are also reduced when they know that they will not be credited for the attack. Rather, the media attention will be *diffused* by actively discussing several possible perpetrators. Such a reaction effectively undermines one of the major reasons for undertaking terrorist activities.

The application of the rational choice approach offers avenues for anti-terrorism policies superior to deterrence. They are effective in dissuading potential terrorists from attacking. All of them are based on the notion that a positive approach is preferable to one based on the use of force. A *positive approach* has significant advantages over coercive anti-terrorist policies based on negative sanctions. The most important are:

- Due to the greater number of outside opportunities, a person's dependence on the terrorist group is reduced. Exit is facilitated and re-integration back into society is possible. Such flexibility is important in view of the fact that there is no such thing as a 'terrorist'. Rather, history has taught us that: 'My terrorist is your freedom fighter'. This being the case, terrorists should be given positive incentives to refrain from violent action and to pursue their goals by peaceful means within the political process. A positive approach creates tensions between the leaders, the rank and file, and active and passive supporters of the terrorist movement. Nobody knows who will succumb to the outside attractions and leave the group. This diminishes the effectiveness of the terrorist group.

- The interaction between the terrorists and all other people and groups is turned into a positive sum interaction in which all parties benefit. The chances of finding a peaceful solution are greatly improved. It invites consideration of what might benefit the other side instead of only seeking ways and means of destroying it. The mutually beneficial interaction created is possibly the strongest argument in favour of the positive approach.

The positive approach championed here is not the only possible strategy, nor does it always work. But the favourable features clearly prevail.

SUGGESTED FURTHER READING

The learning process on the part of terrorist organisations adapting technologically and organisationally to new circumstances is treated in:

Wilkinson, Paul (2000). *Terrorism Versus Democracy: The Liberal State Response.* London: Frank Cass.

Terrorists have even been attributed 'operational ingenuity':

Lesser, Ian O., Bruce Hoffman, John Arquilla, David F. Ronfeldt, Michele Zanini and Brian Michael Jensen (1999). *Countering the New Terrorism.* Santa Monica, CA: Rand Corporation.

The analysis of the incentives of the government and the various groups to undertake and support deterrence and positive anti-terrorist policies is based on Public Choice analysis. See, for example:

Mueller, Dennis C. (ed.) (1997). *Perspectives on Public Choice.* Cambridge: Cambridge University Press.
Mueller, Dennis C. (2003b). *Public Choice III.* Cambridge: Cambridge University Press.

The use of torture by several democratic countries (among them the United States, Israel, Britain and France) is documented in a special report on torture in:

The Economist (2003). 'Ends, Means and Barbarity'. January 11: 20–2.

Deterrence by coercion as the only anti-terrorist policy is discussed in:

Schmid, Alex P. and Ronald D. Crelinsten (eds) (1993). *Western Responses to Terrorism*. London: Frank Cass.

Even the most recent academic analyses of terrorism focus on coercion and neglect positive approaches. See, for instance:

Sandler, Todd (2003). 'Collective Action and Transnational Terrorism'. *World Politics* **26**: 779–802.

The 'rally around the flag' effect is empirically documented, for instance, in:

Nacos, Brigitte L. (1994). *Terrorism and the Media*. New York: Columbia University Press.

The 'macho' attitude, working in favour of using coercive deterrence, is discussed in:

Baldwin, David A. (1971). 'The Power of Positive Sanctions'. *World Politics* **24** (1): 19–38.

The role of the military in shaping anti-terrorist policy is highlighted by:

Wilkinson, Paul (2000). *Terrorism Versus Democracy: The Liberal State Response*. London: Frank Cass, Chapter 6.

An analysis of the features and consequences of direct democracy is provided in:

Kirchgässner, Gebhard, Lars Feld and Marcel R. Savioz (1999). *Die direkte Demokratie: Modern, erfolgreich, entwicklungs- und exportfähig*. Basel et al.: Helbing and Lichtenhahn/Vahlen/Beck.

References

Abadie, Alberto and Javier Gardeazabal (2003). 'The Economic Costs of Conflict: A Case Study for the Basque Country'. *American Economic Review* **93** (1): 113–32.

Alexander, Yonah and Richard Latter (eds) (1990). *Terrorism and the Media*. Washington, DC: Brassey's.

Andreoni, James, Brian Erard and Jonathan Feinstein (1998). 'Tax Compliance'. *Journal of Economic Literature* **76**: 818–60.

Arce M., G. Daniel and T. Sandler (2003). 'An Evolutionary Game Approach to Fundamentalism and Conflict'. *Journal of Institutional and Theoretical Economics*, **159** (1): 132–154.

Arquilla, John and David Ronfeldt (2001). *Networks and Netwars: The Future of Terror, Crime, and Militancy*. Santa Monica, CA: Rand Corporation.

Arrow, Kenneth J. (1951). *Social Choice and Individual Values*. New York: John Wiley & Sons.

Atran, Scott (2003). 'Genesis of Suicide Terrorism'. *Science* **299**: 1534–9.

Baldwin, David A. (1971). 'The Power of Positive Sanctions'. *World Politics* **24** (1): 19–38.

Baldwin, David A. (1985). *Economic Statecraft*. Princeton, NJ: Princeton University Press.

Baldwin, David A. (1999). 'The Sanctions Debate and the Logic of Choice'. *International Security* **24** (3): 80–107.

Baumeister, Roy F. and Mark R. Leary (1995). 'The Need to Belong: Desire for Interpersonal Attachments as a Fundamental Human Motivation'. *Psychological Bulletin* **117** (3): 497–529.

Becker, Gary S. (1968). 'Crime and Punishment: An Economic Approach'. *Journal of Political Economy* **76** (2): 169–217.

Becker, Gary S. (1976). *The Economic Approach to Human Behavior*. Chicago: Chicago University Press.

Becker, Gary S. (1996). *Accounting for Tastes*. Cambridge, MA and London: Harvard University Press.

Becker, Gary S. and Kevin M. Murphy (2001a). 'Prosperity Will Rise Out of the Ashes'. *Wall Street Journal*, October 29, 2001.

Becker, Gary S. and Kevin M. Murphy (2001b). *Social Economics*. Cambridge, MA: Harvard University Press.

Berkowitz, B.J. et al. (1972). *Superviolence: The Threat of Mass Destruction Weapons*. Santa Barbara, CA: ADCON Corporation.

Bernauer, Thomas and Dieter Ruloff (eds) (1999). *The Politics of Positive Incentives in Arms Control*. Columbia, SC: University of South Carolina Press.

Bernholz, Peter (1985). *The International Game of Power*. Berlin: Mouton.

Bierstecker, Thomas J. (2002). 'Targeting Terrorist Finances: The New Challenges of Financial Market Globalization'. In Ken Booth and Tim Dunne (eds). *Worlds in Collision: Terror and the Future of Global Order*. London: Palgrave: 74–84.

Bird, Richard M. (1986). *Federal Finance in Comparative Perspective*. Toronto: Canadian Tax Foundation.

Blomquist, Glenn C., Mark C. Berger and John P. Hoehn (1988). 'New Estimates of the Quality of Life in Urban Areas'. *American Economic Review* **78** (1): 89–107.

Bohnet, Iris and Bruno S. Frey (1999). 'Social Distance and Other-regarding Behavior in Dictator Games: Comment'. *American Economic Review* **89** (1): 335–9.

Boulding, Kenneth E. (1962). *Conflict and Defense*. New York: Harper & Row.

Boulding, Kenneth E. (1973). *The Economy of Love and Fear*. Belmont, CA: Wadsworth.

Brauer, Jurgen (2002). 'On the Economics of Terrorism' *Phi Kappa Phi Forum* **82** (2).

Breton, Albert and Silvana Dalmazzone (2002). 'Information Control, Loss of Autonomy, and the Emergence of Political Extremism'. In Albert Breton, Gianluigi Galeotti, Pierre Salmon and Ronald Wintrobe (eds). *Political Extremism and Rationality*. New York: Cambridge University Press, pp. 44–66.

Brown, Jeffrey R., Randall S. Krozner and Brian H. Jenn (2002). 'Federal Terrorism Risk Insurance'. *National Tax Journal* **55** (3): 647–657.

Buchanan, James M. (1991). *Constitutional Economics*. Oxford: Basil Blackwell.

Buchanan, James M. and Gordon Tullock (1962). *The Calculus of*

Consent. Logical Foundations of Constitutional Democracy. Ann Arbor, MI: University of Michigan Press.

Byman, Daniel L. and Matthew C. Waxman (2002). *The Dynamics of Coercion. American Foreign Policy and the Limits of Military Power*. Cambridge: Cambridge University Press.

Cameron, Samuel (1988). 'The Economics of Crime Deterrence: A Survey of Theory and Evidence'. *Kyklos* **41**: 301–23.

Carr, Caleb (2002). *The Lessons of Terror. A History of Warfare against Civilians: Why It Has Always Failed and Why It Will Fail Again*. New York: Random House.

Chalk, Peter (1995). 'The Liberal Democratic Response to Terrorism'. *Terrorism and Political Violence* **7** (4): 10–44.

Chang, Nancy (2002). *Silencing Political Dissent. How Post-September 11 Anti-terrorism Measures Threaten Our Civil Liberties*. New York: Seven Stories Press.

Coase, Ronald (1960). 'The Problem of Social Cost'. *Journal of Law and Economics* **3**: 1–45.

Coase, Ronald (1988). *The Firm, the Market, and the Law*. Chicago: Chicago University Press.

Cole, David and James X. Dempsey (2002). *Terrorism and the Constitution. Sacrificing Civil Liberties in the Name of National Security*. New York: The New Press.

Collier, Paul and Anke Hoeffler (2001). 'Greed and Grievance in Civil War'. Policy Research Working Paper 2355, World Bank.

Congleton, Roger D. (2002). 'Terrorism, Interest-group Politics, and Public Policy: Curtailing Criminal Modes of Political Speech' *Independent Review* **7** (1): 47–67.

Cooter, Robert D. (2000). *The Strategic Constitution*. Princeton, NJ: Princeton University Press.

Cortright, David (1997). *The Price of Peace. Incentives and International Conflict Prevention*. Lanham, MD: Rowman & Littlefield.

Crelinsten, Ronald D. (1990). 'Terrorism and the Media: Problems, Solutions and Counterproblems'. In David A. Charters (ed). *Democratic Response to International Terrorism*. Ardsley-on-Hudson, New York: Transatlantic Publishers, pp. 267–307.

Crelinsten, Ronald D. and Denis Szabo (1979). *Hostage Taking*. Lexington, KY: Lexington Books.

Crenshaw, Martha (2001). 'Terrorism'. In: Neil J. Smelser and Paul B. Baltes (eds). *International Encyclopedia of the Social and Behavioral Sciences*, Vol. 23. Amsterdam: Pergamon, pp. 15604–6.

Dahl, Robert A. and Charles L. Lindblom (1953). *Politics, Economics and Welfare*. New York: Harper.

Dawes, Robyn M. (1988). *Rational Choice in an Uncertain World*. San Diego, CA and New York: Harcourt, Brace, Jovanovich.

Deci, Edward L. and Richard M. Ryan (1985). *Intrinsic Motivation and Self-determination in Human Behavior*. New York: Plenum Press.

Diamond, Peter A. and Jerry A. Hausman (1994). 'Contingent Valuation: Is Some Number Better than No Number?' *Journal of Economic Perspectives* **8** (4): 45–64.

Downs, George W. and David M. Rocke (1994). 'Conflict, Agency, and Gambling for Resurrection: The Principal–Agent Problem Goes to War'. *American Journal of Political Science* **38**: 362–80.

Drakos, Konstantinos and Ali M. Kutan (2003). 'Regional Effects of Terrorism on Tourism in Three Mediterranean Countries'. *Journal of Conflict Resolution* **47** (5): 621–641.

Drezner, Daniel W. (1999). *The Sanctions Paradox. Economic Statecraft and International Relations*. Cambridge: Cambridge University Press.

Drezner, Daniel W. (1999–2000). 'The Trouble with Carrots: Transactions Costs, Conflict Expectations, and Economic Inducements'. *Security Studies* **9** (1&2): 188–218.

The Economist (2003). 'Ends, Means and Barbarity'. January 11: 20–22.

Elliott, Kimberly Ann and Gary Clyde Hufbauer (1999). 'Same Song, Same Refrain? Economic Sanctions in the 1990s'. *American Economic Review* **89** (2): 403–8.

Enders, Walter and Todd Sandler (1991). 'Causality Between Transnational Terrorism and Tourism: The Case of Spain'. *Terrorism* **14**: 49–58.

Enders, Walter and Todd Sandler (1993). 'The Effectiveness of Antiterrorism Policies: A Vector-Autoregression-Intervention Analysis'. *American Political Science Review* **87** (4): 829–44.

Enders, Walter and Todd Sandler (1996). 'Terrorism and Foreign Direct Investment in Spain and Greece'. *Kyklos* **49** (3): 331–52.

Enders, Walter and Todd Sandler (1999). 'Transnational Terrorism in the Post-Cold War Era'. *International Studies Quarterly* **43** (1): 145–67.

Enders, Walter and Todd Sandler (2000). 'Is Transnational Terrorism

Becoming More Threatening? A Time-series Investigation'. *Journal of Conflict Resolution* **44** (3): 307–32.

Enders, Walter and Todd Sandler (2002). 'Patterns of Transnational Terrorism, 1970–99: Alternative Time Series Estimates'. *International Studies Quarterly* **46**: 145–65.

Enders, Walter and Todd Sandler (2003). 'What Do We Know about the Substitution Effect in Transnational Terrorism'. In Andrew Silke and Gaetano Ilardi (eds). *Terrorism Research: Trends, Achievements and Failures.* London: Frank Cass.

Enders, Walter, Gerald F. Parise and Todd Sandler (1992). 'A Time-series Analysis of Transnational Terrorism: Trends and Cycles'. *Defence Economics* **3** (4): 305–20.

Enders, Walter, Todd Sandler and Jon Cauley (1990a). 'Assessing the Impact of Terrorist-thwarting Policies: An Intervention Time Series Approach'. *Defence Economics* **2** (1): 1–18.

Enders, Walter, Todd Sandler and Jon Cauley (1990b). 'UN Conventions, Technology and Retaliation in the Fight Against Terrorism: An Econometric Evaluation'. *Terrorism and Political Violence* **2** (1): 83–105.

Enders, Walter, Todd Sandler and Gerald F. Parise (1992). 'An Econometric Analysis of the Impact of Terrorism on Tourism'. *Kyklos* **45** (4): 531–54.

Falk, Richard (2003). *The Great Terror War.* New York and Northampton, MA: Olive Branch Press.

Fehr, Ernst and Simon Gächter (1998). 'Reciprocity and Economics. The Economic Implications of Homo Reciprocans'. *European Economic Review* **42**: 845–59.

Fehr, Ernst, Urs Fischbacher and Simon Gächter (2002). 'Strong Reciprocity, Human Cooperation and the Enforcement of Social Norms'. *Human Nature* **13**: 1–25.

Ferrero, Mario (2002). 'Radicalization as a Reaction to Failure: An Economic Model of Islamic Extremism'. Department of Public Policy and Public Choice Working Paper No. 33, University of Eastern Piedmont, Italy.

Ferrero, Mario (2003). 'Martyrdom Contracts'. Mimeo, Department of Public Policy and Public Choice, University of Eastern Piedmont, Italy.

Fleming, Peter (2001). 'International Terrorism: Attributes of Terrorist Events 1992–1998. (ITERATE 5 update)'. Mimeo.

Frey, Bruno S. (1983). *Democratic Economic Policy.* Oxford: Blackwell.

Frey, Bruno S. (1984). *International Political Economics*. Oxford: Blackwell.

Frey, Bruno S. (1997). *Not Just for The Money. An Economic Theory of Personal Motivation*. Cheltenham, UK and Brookfield, USA: Edward Elgar.

Frey, Bruno S. (1999). *Economics as a Science of Human Behaviour*, 2nd revised and extended edn. Boston and Dordrecht: Kluwer.

Frey, Bruno S. (2001). *Inspiring Economics: Human Motivation in Political Economy*. Cheltenham, UK and Northampton, USA: Edward Elgar.

Frey, Bruno S. and Reiner Eichenberger (1999). *The New Democratic Federalism for Europe: Functional Overlapping and Competing Jurisdictions*. Cheltenham, UK: Edward Elgar.

Frey, Bruno S. and Simon Luechinger (2003a). 'How to Fight Terrorism: Alternatives to Deterrence'. *Defence and Peace Economics* **14** (4): 237–49.

Frey, Bruno S. and Simon Luechinger (2003). 'Measuring Terrorism'. IEW Working Paper No. 171, University of Zurich.

Frey, Bruno S., Simon Luechinger and Alois Stutzer (2004). 'Valuing Public Goods: The Life Satisfaction Approach'. IEW Working Paper No. 184, University of Zurich.

Frey, Bruno S., Felix Oberholzer-Gee and Reiner Eichenberger (1996). 'The Old Lady Visits Your Backyard: A Tale of Morals and Markets'. *Journal of Political Economy* **104** (6): 1297–313; reprinted in Frey, Bruno S. (2001). *Inspiring Economics: Human Motivation in Political Economy*. Cheltenham, UK and Northampton, USA: Edward Elgar.

Frey, Bruno S. and Alois Stutzer (2002). *Happiness and Economics. How the Economy and Institutions Affect Human Well-being*. Princeton, NJ: Princeton University Press.

Friedman, Thomas (2002). *Longitudes and Attitudes*. New York: Farrar, Strauss, Giroux.

Galtung, Johan (1965). 'On the Meaning of Nonviolence'. *Journal of Peace Research* **2** (3): 228–57.

Gentzkow, Matthew and Jesse M. Shapiro (2004). 'Media, Education, and Anti-Americanism in the Muslim World'. *Journal of Economic Perspectives*, forthcoming.

George, Alexander L. and William E. Simon (eds) (1994). *The Limits of Coercive Diplomacy*. Boulder, CO: Westview Press.

Glaeser, Edward L. (2002). 'The Political Economy of Hatred'.

NBER Working Paper No. 9171, Cambridge, MA: National Bureau of Economic Research.

Glaeser, Edward L. and Jesse M. Shapiro (2001). 'Cities and Warfare: The Impact of Terrorism on Urban Form'. *Journal of Urban Economics* **51**: 205–24.

Habermas, Jürgen (1992). *Faktizität und Geltung: Beiträge zur Diskurstheorie des Rechts und des demokratischen Rechtsstaates.* Frankfurt: Suhrkamp.

Hardin, Russel (2002). 'The Crippled Epistemology of Extremism'. In Albert Breton, Gianluigi Galeotti, Pierre Salmon and Ronald Wintrobe (eds). *Political Extremism and Rationality.* New York: Cambridge University Press, pp. 3–22.

Harmon, Christopher C. (2000). *Terrorism Today.* London: Frank Cass.

Hess, Gregory D. (2003). 'The Economic Welfare Cost of Conflict: An Empirical Assessment'. CESifo Working Paper No. 852.

Hirschman, Albert O. (1964). 'The Stability of Neutralism: A Geometrical Note'. *American Economic Review* **54** (2): 94–100.

Hirshleifer, Jack (1978). 'Natural Economy versus Political Economy'. *Journal of Social and Biological Structures* **1** (4): 319–37.

Hirshleifer, Jack (2001). *The Dark Side of the Force: Economic Foundations of Conflict Theory.* Cambridge: Cambridge University Press.

Hoffman, Bruce (1998). *Inside Terrorism.* New York: Columbia University Press.

Huang, Reyko (2001). 'Mounting Costs of the Financial War Against Terrorism'. Mimeo, CDI Terrorism Project [Internet: http://www.cdi.org/terrorism/financial2-pr.cfm].

Hudson, Rex A. (1999). *The Sociology and Psychology of Terrorism. Who Becomes a Terrorist and Why?* Washington, DC: Federal Research Division, Library of Congress [Internet: http://www.fas. org/irp/frd.html].

Hufbauer, Gary Clyde and Barbara Oegg (2000). 'Targeted Sanctions: A Policy Alternative?' *Law and Policy in International Business* **32** (1): 11–20.

Hufbauer, Gary Clyde, Jeffrey J. Schott and Kimberly Ann Elliott (1990). *Economic Sanctions Reconsidered: History and Current Policy*, 2nd edn. Washington, DC: Institute for International Economics.

Hufbauer, Gary Clyde, Jeffrey J. Schott and Barbara Oegg (2001).

'Using Sanctions to Fight Terrorism'. Mimeo, Institute for International Economics [Internet: http://www.iie.com/policy-briefs/news 01–11.htm].

International Monetary Fund (2001). 'How Has September 11 Influenced the Global Economy?' *World Economic Outlook*, Chapter 11.

Jenkins, Brian M. (2000). Opening Address at the Conference on Terrorism and Beyond organised by the Oklahoma City National Memorial Institute for the Prevention of Terrorism, April 14, 2000 [Internet: http://www.mipt.org/jenkins-ctb.asp].

Kaempfer, William and Anton Lowenberg (1992). *International Economic Sanctions.* Boulder, CO: Westview Press.

Keohane, Nathaniel O. and Richard Zeckhauser (2003). 'The Ecology of Terror Defense'. *Journal of Risk and Uncertainty* **26** (2–3): 201–229.

Kirchgässner, Gebhard (2000). *Homo Oeconomicus: Das ökonomische Modell individuellen Verhaltens und seine Anwendung in den Wirtschafts- und Sozialwissenschaften*, 2nd edn. Tübingen: Mohr (Siebeck).

Kirchgässner, Gebhard, Lars Feld and Marcel R. Savioz (1999). *Die direkte Demokratie: Modern, erfolgreich, entwicklungs- und exportfähig.* Basel et al.: Helbing and Lichtenhahn/ Vahlen/ Beck.

Konrad, Kai A. (2002). 'Terrorism and the State'. WZB, Social Science Research Center Berlin Discussion Papers.

Krueger, Alan B. and Jitka Maleckovà (2003). 'Education, Poverty and Terrorism: Is There a Causal Connection?' *Journal of Economic Perspectives* **17** (4): 119–144'.

Kushner, Harvey W. (ed.) (1998). *The Future of Terrorism. Violence in the New Millenium.* London: Sage.

Landes, William A. (1978). 'An Economic Study of US Aircraft Hijackings, 1961–1976'. *Journal of Law and Economics* **21** (1): 1–31.

Lapan, Harvey E. and Todd Sandler (1988). 'To Bargain or Not to Bargain: That Is the Question'. *American Economic Review* **78** (2): 16–21.

Laqueur, Walter (1977). *Terrorism.* London: Weidenfeld and Nicolson.

Lee, Dwight R. (1988). 'Free Riding and Paid Riding in the Fight Against Terrorism'. *American Economic Review* **78**: 22–6.

Lesser, Ian O., Bruce Hoffman, John Arquilla, David F. Ronfeldt, Michele Zanini and Brian Michael Jensen (1999). *Countering the New Terrorism.* Santa Monica, CA: Rand Corporation.

Levy, Jack S. (1996), 'Loss aversion, framing and bargaining: the implications of prospect theory for international conflict', *International Political Science Review*, **17** (2): 179–95.

Levy, Jack S. (1997). 'Prospect Theory, Rational Choice, and International Relations'. *International Studies Quarterly* **41**: 87–112.

Mickolus, Edward F. (1982). *International Terrorism: Attributes of Terrorist Events 1968–1977. (ITERATE 2)*. Ann Arbor, MI: Inter-University Consortium for Political and Social Research.

Mickolus, Edward F., Todd Sandler, Jean M. Murdock and Peter Fleming (1989). *International Terrorism: Attributes of Terrorist Events, 1978–1987. (ITERATE 3)*. Dunn Loring, VA: Vinyard Software.

Mickolus, Edward F., Todd Sandler, Jean M. Murdock and Peter Fleming (1993). *International Terrorism: Attributes of Terrorist Events, 1988–1991. (ITERATE 4)*. Dunn Loring, VA: Vinyard Software.

Miron, Jeffrey A. and Jeffrey Zweifel (1995). 'The Economic Case Against Drug Prohibition'. *Journal of Economic Perspectives* **9** (4): 175–92.

Mueller, Dennis C. (1996). *Constitutional Democracy*. New York: Oxford University Press.

Mueller, Dennis C. (ed.) (1997). *Perspectives on Public Choice*. Cambridge: Cambridge University Press.

Mueller, Dennis C. (2003a). 'Rights and Citizenship in a World of Global Terrorism'. Mimeo, Department of Economics, University of Vienna.

Mueller, Dennis C. (2003b). *Public Choice III*. Cambridge: Cambridge University Press.

Nacos, Brigitte L. (1994). *Terrorism and the Media*. New York: Columbia University Press.

Navarro, Peter and Aron Spencer (2001). 'September 2001: Assessing the Costs of Terrorism'. *Milken Institute Review* **2**: 16–31.

Nitsch, Volker and Dieter Schumacher (2004). 'Terrorism and International Trade: An Empirical Investigation'. *European Journal of Political Economy*, forthcoming. Paper prepared for the workshop on The Economic Consequences of Global Terrorism, organised by DIW Berlin, June 14–15, 2002.

Oates, Wallace E. (1991). *Studies in Fiscal Federalism*. Aldershot: Edward Elgar.

Osterloh, Margit and Sandra Rota (2002). 'Open Source Software Production. The Magic Cauldron?' Mimeo, University of Zurich.

O'Sullivan, John (1986). 'Media Publicity Causes Terrorism'. In Bonnie Szumski (ed.). *Terrorism: Opposing Viewpoints.* St Paul, MN: Greenhaven Press, pp. 69–74.

Pape, Robert A. (1997). 'Why Economic Sanctions Do Not Work'. *International Security* **22** (2): 90–136.

Pape, Robert A. (1998). 'Why Economic Sanctions Still Do Not Work'. *International Security* **23** (1): 66–77.

Parry, Albert (1976). *Terrorism. From Robespierre to Arafat.* New York: Vanguard Press.

Pieth, Mark (ed.) (2003). *Financing Terrorism.* Boston, Dordrecht and London: Kluwer.

Pizam, Abraham and Ginger Smith (2000). 'Tourism and Terrorism: A Quantitative Analysis of Major Terrorist Acts and Their Impact on Tourism Destinations'. *Tourism Economics* **6** (2): 123–38.

Portney, Kent E. (1991). *Siting Hazardous Waste Treatment Facilities: The NIMBY Syndrome.* New York: Auburn House.

Quillen, Chris (2000). 'State-sponsored WMD Terrorism: A Growing Threat?' Mimeo, Terrorism Research Center [Internet: www.terrorism.com].

Rathbone, Anne and Charles K. Rowley (2002). 'Terrorism'. *Public Choice* **111** (1–2): 9–18.

Rawls, John (1971). *A Theory of Justice.* Cambridge, MA: Harvard University Press.

Rom, Pierre (2000). *La longue histoire de la question jurassienne: étude d'un engagé en politique sur les fonds historiques, culturels et topographiques.* Urtenen, CH: Pierre Rom.

Russell, Charles and Bowman H. Miller (1977). 'Profile of a Terrorist'. *Terrorism: An International Journal* **1** (1): 17–34.

Sally, David (1995). 'Conversation and Cooperation in Social Dilemmas. A Meta-analysis of Experiments from 1958 to 1992'. *Rationality and Society* **7** (1): 58–92.

Sandler, Todd (1997). *Global Challenges.* Cambridge: Cambridge University Press.

Sandler, Todd (2003). 'Collective Action and Transnational Terrorism'. *World Politics* **26**: 779–802.

Sandler, Todd and Walter Enders (2004). 'An Economic Perspective on Transnational Terrorism'. *European Journal of Political Economy*, forthcoming.

Sandler, Todd and Harvey E. Lapan (1988). 'The Calculus of Dissent: An Analysis of Terrorists' Choice of Targets'. *Synthese* **76:** 245–61.

Schelling, Thomas C. (1960). *The Strategy of Conflict.* Oxford: Oxford University Press.

Schelling, Thomas C. (1966). *Arms and Influence.* New Haven, CT: Yale University Press.

Schelling, Thomas C. (1984). *Choice and Consequence: Perspectives of an Errant Economist.* Cambridge, MA: Harvard University Press.

Schelling, Thomas C. (1991). 'What Purposes Can "International Terrorism" Serve?' In Raymond G. Frey and Christopher W. Morris (eds). *Violence, Terrorism, and Justice.* Cambridge: Cambridge University Press, pp. 18–32.

Schmid, Alex P. and Ronald D. Crelinsten (eds) (1993). *Western Responses to Terrorism.* London: Frank Cass.

Schmid, Alex P. and Albert J. Jongman (1988). *Political Terrorism: A New Guide to Actors, Authors, Concepts, Data Bases, Theories, and Literature.* New Brunswick, NJ: Transaction Books.

Schneider, Friedrich (2004). 'Money for Terror: The Hidden Financial Flows of Islamic Terrorist Organizations', *Defence and Peace Economics*, forthcoming.

Selten, Reinhard (1977). 'A Simple Game Model of Kidnapping'. In Rudolf Henn and Otto Moeschlin (eds). *Mathematical Economics and Game Theory: Lecture Notes in Economics and Mathematical Systems,* Vol. 141. Berlin: Springer, pp. 139–56.

Sen, Amartya K. (1970). *Collective Choice and Social Welfare.* Republished, Amsterdam: North Holland (1979), San Francisco, CA: Holden-Day.

Stern, Jessica (1999). *The Ultimate Terrorists.* Cambridge, MA and London: Harvard University Press.

Takács, Károly (2001). 'Structural Embeddedness and Intergroup Conflict'. *Journal of Conflict Resolution* **45** (6): 743–69.

Taylor, Maxwell and Ethel Quayle (1994). *The Terrorist Lives.* London and Washington, DC: Brassey's.

Tollison, Robert D. and Thomas D. Willet (1979). 'An Economic Theory of Mutually Advantageous Issue Linkages in International Negotiations'. *International Organization* **33** (4): 425–49.

Tololyan, Khachig (2001). 'Cultural Narrative and the Motivation of a Terrorist'. In David C. Rapoport (ed.). *Inside Terrorist Organizations.* London: Frank Cass, pp. 217–33.

Tullock, Gordon (1974). *The Social Dilemma. The Economics of War and Revolution*. Blacksburg, VA: University Publications.

US State Department (various years). *Patterns of Global Terrorism*. Washington, DC: US Department of State.

US State Department, title 22 of the United States Code, section 265f(d)[Def. Terrorism].

Van Beest, Ilja, Henk Wilke and Eric van Dijk (2004). 'The Interplay of Self-interest and Equity in Coalition Formation'. *European Journal of Social Psychology*, forthcoming.

Van Bergeijk, Peter A.G. (1994). *Economic Diplomacy, Trade, and Commercial Policy: Positive and Negative Sanctions in a New World Order*. Aldershot: Edward Elgar.

Viscusi, W. Kip and Richard J. Zeckhauser (2003). 'Sacrificing Civil Liberties to Reduce Terrorism Risks'. *Journal of Risk and Uncertainty* **26** (2–3): 99–120.

von Hayek, Friedrich A. (1978). 'Competition as Discovery Procedure'. In Friedrich A. von Hayek (ed.). *New Studies in Philosophy, Politics, Economics and the History of Ideas*. London: Routledge and Kegan Paul, pp. 119–30.

Walkenhorst, Peter and Nora Dihel (2002). 'Trade Impacts of the Terrorist Attacks of 11 September 2001: Quantitative Assessment'. Paper prepared for the workshop on The Economic Consequences of Terrorism, organised by the DIW Berlin, June 14–15, 2002.

Wieviorka, Michel (1993). *The Making of Terrorism*. Chicago and London: University of Chicago Press.

Wilkinson, Paul (2000). *Terrorism Versus Democracy: The Liberal State Response*. London: Frank Cass.

Williamson, Oliver E. (1985). *The Economic Institutions of Capitalism. Firms, Markets, Relational Contracting*. New York: Free Press.

Wintrobe, Ronald (2002a). 'Can Suicide Bombers be Rational?' Paper prepared for the workshop on The Economic Consequences of Global Terrorism, organised by DIW Berlin, June 14–15, 2002.

Wintrobe, Ronald (2002b). 'Leadership and Passion in Extremist Politics'. In Albert Breton, Gianluigi Galeotti, Pierre Salmon and Ronald Wintrobe (eds). *Political Extremism and Rationality*. New York: Cambridge University Press, pp. 23–43.

Zambrano, Eduardo (2001). 'An Emergency Introduction to the Economics of Terrorism'. Mimeo, Mendoza College of Business [Internet: http://www.nd.edu/~ezambran/sept11/ Introd.pdf].

Name Index

Subject Index